Anchor's Aweigh

Des Sleightholme

Illustrations by the author

Adlard Coles Nautical
London

Contents

Published 1997 by Adlard Coles Nautical
an imprint of A & C Black (Publishers) Ltd
35 Bedford Row, London WC1R 4JH

Copyright © J D Sleightholme 1997

ISBN 0-7136-4812-0

A CIP catalogue record for this book is available from the
British Library.

Set in 11½/12½ Plantin
Printed and bound in Great Britain by
The Cromwell Press, Melksham, Wiltshire

Foreword by Old Harry

The first time I met the author he was in short pants and a little sailor suit, which struck me as odd, him being thirty-five and growin' a beard.

I was sat in the cockpit of *Ferret,* my old converted cockle-grubber, one sunny mornin', not a breath o' wind and the ebb well away, enjoyin' a nice mug o' tay. I do recall that it was the first time I'd tried a tea bag instead o'a tea pot and it were leakin' something shockin'.

Well he come driftin' by on this upturned table he was usin' as a raft. It was gaff rigged on all four legs. I called out, 'I'll bet that's stable.'

He never spoke. It were another six hours afore he come a'driftin' back again on the next flood.

'Yes,' he says, 'Yes, that's a table,' and he drifted on up-river.

Well just afore supper I see him come driftin' back on the ebb again. I had a nice bit o' pig's cheek a'boilin' away. I called out, 'I see you've got cabriole legs.'

He never answered, just went driftin' on by. He were back again in the early hours, on the next flood. The great panoply o' the star-studded heavens shed a fitful light o'er the scene.

'No,' he says, 'them's my varicose veins.'

He always was a chatterbox though.

Well I taught that lad all I know. I introduced him to the Navigator's Ancient Art, the Cock and Bull's two-finger Fred and the barmaid at the Dog and Bucket. I taught him how to use a chart, how to make cocked hats, lampshades an' how to make a grecian frieze round the bottom.

I was an instrumental part o' that lad's future – I played fiddle while he went round with the cap. I taught him seamanship to the highest level and how to execute a running moor. I can fairly claim to have started him off on his career. He careered down the high street into the Chinese takeaway. I should have warned him about them brakes. It cost him five number fours wi' extra noodles to go.

To the readers of this book then, just follow in the author's footsteps, which is them muddy ones leadin' up the slip to the bus stop, and you won't go far.

Signed Old Harry **X**

Introduction

Cruising can alter your life

You'll be a different person
(a very much worse-un)
If you go to sea in a yacht.
'But how much will it cost?'
I hear you riposte.
At a rough estimation THE LOT.

Perhaps we all have a secret yearning for the gypsy way of life or for the vast open spaces of the desert nomad, the nights under a canopy of stars, munching sheep's eyes in a reeking and verminous camel-hair tent.

First we should consider what we mean by 'cruising'. Stop any man-in-the-street and say, 'Would you like to come for a cruise with me?' As the echo of his pounding boots dies away in the distance, it becomes plain that there are other concepts of cruising.

To most people it is synonymous with quoits and shipboard romances. The warm tropical nights, the moonlight, a glittering wake, a handsome companion, wearing your little black frock with the matching bag.

Your dictionary may define cruising as 'sailing about without precise destination' (a fair description of novice navigation). In the context of this book, however, it means proceeding at a leisurely speed in pursuit of pleasure, while pitting one's strength, nerve and stamina in the achievement of a watery goal.

Seagoing offers great opportunities for self-improve-

ment. It enables the tyro to make something of him/
herself (implying a kit of parts and a frowning study of
the instructions). It offers rich rewards in terms of
responsibility as a skipper and builds up a new air of confidence. The eye takes on a steely glitter, there is a new
firmness about the jaw, the lips are drawn into a thin line
that brooks no argument – and that's just the lady-wife.

A skipper becomes a decision-maker. 'We *will* be
anchoring in 15 m, fn snd and md!' he bellows above the
howl of the tempest. He catches her eye. '. . . Or berthing
in the marina, unlimited ht wtr and that boutique with
those very reasonable-little-denim-sun-frocks,' he
amends quickly.

The yacht owner gains a certain standing in sailing circles. It provides an *entrée* to a professional world hitherto
denied the layman.

Let us take the medical profession, for example. Your
GP may be a fellow owner. Ordinarily a surgery visit
would be totally impersonal and conversationally barren.
He/she would pretend to be writing busily as you enter.

'Lie-on-the-couch-you-may-leave-your-socks-on,'
he/she intones, making a concession to modesty and flex-
ing the fingers. Somewhere between patella and peri-
toneum recognition dawns. 'I see you've got a little
Twister these days then,' he/she notes, diagnostically
(and disturbingly). These little personal touches are
important.

This camaraderie is general thoughout the profes-
sions. 'Go in peace my son,' says the parish priest, after
adding a swingeing penance. 'What have you got on
your bottom this year?'

A visit to the bank manager (radiating reliability, club
tie and clean vest) is not perhaps always as genial. 'I only
wish I could see my way clear . . .' he mourns, wagging
his dewlaps, hinting at a trip up the mast with the binos.
'. . . and I wish *I* could afford to fit in-mast reefing,' he
rounds off waspishly, pointedly getting to his feet.

The rising young executive may find an opportunity
for social intercourse with influential people via a

shared interest. Ordinarily the golf course is the venue for creepers.

'Oh hard luck, sir!' cries young Rodney from Bought Ledger Dept, watching 'sir' cock up a six inch putt. He then holes his own twenty-footer. Sir will remember him for a very, very long time. The marina men's ablutions offer a similar chance to 'make his number'.

Cruising is for the whole family to enjoy and it will also widen your circle of friends. And boat ownership solves the package holiday problem for ever more. Once you stump up for a thirty thousand quid mortgage just to get from Ramsgate to Calais the only package you'll be able to afford is the cheese-and-tomato sandwiches for a day excursion to Ostende.

Youngsters really take to cruising. They take their ghetto-blasters, drum kits and mountain bikes, which means widening the forehatch. 'You're-always-picking-on-me' Sandra takes over the loo and vanity facilities.

Teenagers get an opportunity to 'find themselves' – a rare treat for parents long accustomed to them shambling around in a moronic daze with their shirts hanging out. Youngsters will return from their first cruise with a new aim in life[1].

The reader is urged to read Chapter Three, Why not charter?, with close attention prior to embarking upon boat ownership. The novice might be well advised to sail as paying crew on some charter yacht, to get a 'taste of the sea'. After all, 'sea' is something he/she is likely to taste a lot of as a supplement to the soggy Cream Cracker scupper-supper which is the usual on-passage sustenance for first timers.

In most cases it is the bread-winner of the family who volunteers (with typical unselfishness) to go on such a holiday alone, later reporting back to the family with a detailed and accurate account (plus 400 glossy prints and straw donkey).

---

[1] To distance themselves from cruising as far and as fast as possible.

Looking the part

Should the family decide to buy a boat, every effort should be made to 'look the part' thus concealing their novice status and providing 'protective colouration' much in the manner of helpless nestlings merging with their leafy surroundings.

Endeavour to amuse your friends with nautical comments made about droll every-day situations. For instance if mother-in-law's bottom gets stuck in her cane chair the humorist might cry 'Ahoy there, let go aft and full ahead both'. Or 'Time for four rolls and a storm jib, eh parson!' – apropos the embarrassing and audible little accident as the vicar mounts his pulpit.

These mirth-provoking remarks must not get out of hand. When the company Chairman's hairpiece gets trapped in the lift door, for instance, the young executive is best advised to ignore this distressing accident, and not cry out, as did one (now company car-less) fellow, 'Ho, ho, ho, topsail carried away then, Sir?'

One might invite a neighbour in for drinks and interrupt his/her best anecdote by leaping up with a cry of 'My God. We're missing the shipping forecast!' Or take to driving around with a pair of oars on the roof-rack, coming home at midnight on Sunday, exclaiming 'My God, what a flog! She loved it with the flood up her stern!'

While this makes a lasting impression, appearance is even more important. Let us consider what to wear:

Footwear

This should preferably be blue canvas, thoroughly boiled with holes pierced in them so that the big toes can emerge like the heads of small tortoises after hibernation. (Cases are recorded of old ladies trying to tempt them out with lettuce leaves.)

Headgear

A cap can usually be picked up. If bought new, however, simmer in 1 ltr bilge water plus 2 tsp sump oil, and 3 tsp antifouling. Quick-dry with blowlamp. Then drive over it.

Jeans

If new, mix pigeon guano with any good household pollutant, bleach kneecaps, and while still moist fill with sharp sand and beat against wall until cups or 'cusps' form. Continue until these burst.

Sweater

Preferably white(ish). Machine-wash with one pr (cheap) brown and one pr green socks. Set the programme to 'heavily soiled/disgusting'. Follow by two weeks in the dog's bed. The garment should by then have acquired a foul khaki patina and a stain vaguely resembling a map of Rutland grouted with Pedigree Chum.

Oilskins

Find a marina garbage skip, where a choice of foul-weather gear (or foul weathergear) is generally to be had. Choose wisely because there is a lot of rubbish about these days. Wear only when ashore, changing into brand new stuff once out of sight at sea.

Other items

A whistle, hand-bearing compass, mini binoculars etc may be hung around the neck. If you fall overboard this is as good a way of Meeting your Maker as any. The wearing of large sheath knives on the hip can add an aura of 'By heaven I've been out there!' They can also bang ten degrees of deviation on the compass. Wearers of large sheath knives with dodgy sheaths should never leap into an inflatable dinghy with a cry of 'All ashore then, I'm dying for a drink!'

Chapter One

Choosing a boat

For going afloat you must have a boat
Of that there is no denying.
You'd be pushing your luck with a rubber duck
Which only leaves yogic flying

It is tempting to think merely in terms of crew size versus price: how much boat for how much money. This policy can win you a waterborne Wendy House with folk-weave curtains which will sail like a balloon on a string. Conversely, the fast cruiser/racer shaped like a soup-dish and wet as a tinker's cur offers scant solace to a novice crew. Perching them in a row along the weather rail as if poised for a mass-migration is no way to treat sensitive human beings – and we mustn't forget Miriam's chest.

Where will the boat be kept? In shoal waters? This means a shallow bottomed boat, a lifting keel or bilge keels which will allow our small ship to 'dry out', standing straddled like an old woman at a bus stop with sore feet and two bulging bags.

Shoal water sailing offers many modest adventures exploring the shallow and winding creeks and marshes common to such areas. Borne on a fat spring tide our explorers will penetrate far, far inland to the haunts of reed bunting and irate ornithologists, reaching limits rarely sailed, there to stick solidly and immovably like a clock on a mantelpiece for the next month.

The novice might be well advised to buy a popular class of boat secondhand with a view to a quick trade-in having once reached an understanding of what he/she really wants. Such a vessel will be about as exciting as a coffee morning. She will have 'full standing headroom' (an attitude achieved by Man after a few million years of scuttling around on his knuckles) and every drop of water that comes aboard will end up in bed with you as soon as the boat heels. For every owner of such a craft, bored out of his skull and eager to sell, there is another dozen muffins all waving cheques and keen to buy.

Or a choice must be made between the car-wash qualities of the 'performance' boat with a motion like a Chieftain tank on a ploughed field which is 'a joy to handle', as owners will assure you, raising dripping features and blowing out salt, and the boat that sails like a seagoing confessional.

Big enough?

When builders state 'four berths, optional five' they are assuming that the crew will go aboard stark naked, without personal baggage, and that they will all lie down at once, each in his/her personal slot like biscuits in a box of Highland Assortment. The day is not far distant when we will have to be measured for our bunk. '. . . And now the inside left leg, sir . . . !'

An 'optional' crew member is a sort of nomad, and like the new and very unimportant club member, left off the Annual Dinner seating plan by mistake, condemned to drift wraith-like in search of a resting place.

An optional berth is usually the cabin sole between settee berths, where nocturnal wanderers in search of the loo will tip-toe heavily from solar plexus to glottis as if treading grapes.

The berths or bunks aboard a yacht usually serve a double function:

The quarter berth This is located in a plywood tunnel next to a roaring engine and a busy ladder and irrigated by regular bursts of spray. The remaining three-quarters of the berth is given over to the stowage of boathook, fenders, boarding ladder, oars, the baby's potty and the navigator's vast and straining buttocks which block access. Once in the berth and with the navigator *in situ* it will take scaling ladders or an SAS rescue team with stun-grenades to get you out.

Settee berths At sea the leeward settee berth becomes the permanent residence of whoever ate the dodgy *moules marinières*.

The galley being at the after end of a settee berth, do not sleep facing aft otherwise features may become mottled by flying droplets of tomato soup. 'Plague by

Heaven!' father will howl, sending out a PAN PAN MEDICO call.

Forecastle berth Stowage for huge, reeking bags of wet sail, inflatable dinghy, yellow wellies and Norman's ridiculous suitcase which everybody *told* him not to bring. Sleepers must have triangular figures and be alert for the questing boot of crew descending the forehatch ladder.

Pipe cot This is a one-man/woman trampoline. When going to windward in a head sea sleepers (sic) sound like a Royal Marine drum recital.

Root berth This is no more than a canvas shelf above a settee berth whereon the sleeper 'roots' around in search of ease. Access is achieved by placing a foot in the groin of the sleeper below and giving a vigorous upward spring, the sleeper assisting by jerking bolt upright with a cry of 'PAWFFF!'

The galley

Where is it located? Ideally it is next to the hatch thus guaranteeing a steady blast of wind and spray and adjacent to the chart table which provides useful 'putting-down' space.

Has it a two-burner and grill capacity? Many tasty snacks can be reduced to smoking ruin on such a handy little cooker.

Has it an oven? If so, then food can slide from side to side as you tack, producing that toothsome sailing speciality, one side red raw and the other as black as sin. The word 'hardtack' derives from this source, eg that tack upon which biscuit and burner are in contact.

This feature is overcome if our cooker is 'gymballed' or swinging. The cook works with his/her navel or moustache alternately in the stir-fry. If not fully gymballed however, an extra heavy roll brings up the cooker with a wham. Inspect the chart for flying morsels of nourishment. A single lentil (fixed red) could lure a vessel to disaster.

The toilet

At the very heart of our small ship where five people are living in an area comparable to a confessional, the privacy offered by a separate toilet is precious. The 'heads' is the centre of civilisation as we know it. Sanity through sanitation.

In the morning and while at anchor bowed figures clutching spongebags sidle in and out like special agents bent upon clandestine missions.

When 'somebody is in there', etiquette demands that the radio is turned up full and that everybody talks or whistles loudly and together. Occupants endeavour to pump soundlessly and with a delicacy of touch that would not disgrace a concert hall pianist.

It is a well known fact that Miriam won't go near it unless there is a background racket like an armed uprising. Its use at an inappropriate moment (like when father needs it) can be a source of friction.

'Is somebody in there?' comes the stern enquiry.

There is total silence.

'Tch! how long are you going to be in there?'

An inaudible mumble.

'Well we're getting under way!' he triumphs, clumping around. Not only do they get under way but hard on the wind. As the boat heels the mysterious inmate finds himself/herself tipped forward at an angle of 45° and there follows a spell of sanitary gymnastics worthy of Chipperfields.

Inside this modest compartment the mechanical toilet, or 'galloper' as the vulgar may call it, crouches like a sumo wrestler. Above it, sited so that the seat catches blobs of toothpaste, is the tip-up washbasin. This amenity discharges into the toilet bowl which overflows into your slippers – hence the origin of the term 'slipper-bath'.

Underfoot there is a teak grating which imparts a waffle iron pattern to the soles of the feet. Many yachts are equipped with a shower which delivers jets like a heavy dew, automatically shutting off as soon as the user is fully soaped. It reduces the toilet roll to a soggy pap and father to a state of babbling fury.

The fore cabin

This is a small triangular cuddy wherein sleepers lie in a V formation like some form of Celtic burial custom. As feet make contact sleepers groan horribly and commence a bicycling motion, ending up in the foetal position knees-to-chin.

The fore cabin is a sort of knacker's back-yard for junk turfed out from elsewhere aboard. Vast sail bags are constantly being squeezed through the forehatch in a sort of gynaecological theme-play. At sea the anchor on deck pounds like a big bass drum and the chain-pipe or 'naval' pipe (appropriately aimed at the sleeper's midriff) deluges water with the regularity of an automatic urinal flush.

At sea, crew on watch bang in and out all night in dripping oilskins in search of things. It is the only place aboard where man and wife can retire for a furiously whispered row and where teenagers can plot bloody rebellion.

Boat-hunting

A yacht can be bought new at a boat show or from an advertisement in a yachting magazine which shows crews grinning through clenched teeth and waving dementedly, indicating either a state of ecstasy or deep distress.

Alternatively a boat can be bought secondhand or 'used' as the Trade calls it, implying that a flip with a wet cloth is all that is needed to make it as good as new.

The classified ads pages in magazines list both private sales and yacht brokers who bite a fat chunk out of the owner's sale price. The former may reveal the depths of emotion felt by owners, a 'sale of old Dobbin' hint of grim separation.

'Genuine sacrifice!' sobs one owner, hinting at robed and chanting figures waving obsidian ceremonial knives. 'Give-away price, going abroad!' wails another – perhaps gazing mournfully at the receding land of his fathers.

The brokers also use a language which must be translated. They send out muddy-looking photostats of muddy photostats plus brief details of each boat. 'One owner, immaculate condition' refers to the owner not the boat. 'A boat of great character . . .' means rotten as a rustic bench and 'sleeps 5/6' means head-to-foot and anaesthetised. 'Owner seeking larger' must be treated with profound caution. 'Owner seeking lager' might be nearer the mark and indicate some lush with a bilge full of empties and grass growing out of the cockpit cushions.

When visiting a boat show a buyer may have a low price ceiling but it won't prevent him/her from having a bit of a poke around in the attic. Wear a polo-necked sweater to hide the rapid shuttling up and down of the Adam's apple upon noting the price of the super sail-away Show Offers. The salesman whose lofty gaze has already taken cognisance of your pannier pockets stuffed with packed lunch and stand-at-ease trousers, should be shown at once that you are not to be dismissed lightly. Adopt a knowledgeable air. 'Good morning. I see you have an easy entry and a firm buttock line!' might be a typical approach. 'Is your stuffing gland easily accessible?' This will impress the fellow.

Your aim must then be to save face and effect a dignified exit. Look him in the eye continually, remembering to take note of the open forehatch and companionway – as an abrupt and wailing descent of either could affect your credibility. Frown, look up the mast and poke around below. You have no more intention of taking out a £60,000 mortgage than a Fakir might have of stumping up for a Slumberland mattress but you will have him wondering.

'I've put you on my short list and you'll soon be hearing from me!' you might comfort him, with an eerie sense of prophecy, exiting backwards towards the ladder. There is an ornamental rope across the top. You then make an abrupt and wailing descent.

When dealing with a private owner the first requirement is to demoralise him. Adopt an expression of profound disappointment the moment you set eyes on his boat. It is better to visit as one of a pair; you can then hold whispered conversations, punctuated by slow shakes of the head, the sucking of air through the teeth and then glances at your watch.

'What a pity!' you might murmur, 'What a pity. Still, we may as well take a quick look now we're here.'

Your next goal is to find something wrong. An immovable seacock (to be found on all boats) is an excellent target. It's a good idea to open a locker. 'Come and look at this . . .' you invite your companion frown-ingly. Since there will always be something, somewhere, that the owner would rather nobody saw he becomes a plum ripe for picking. You can proceed to undo his ask-ing price like dismantling the Christmas tree.

Shared ownership

Why not share the cost and upkeep of owning a boat with another couple, either as sailing partners or to use the boat turn and turn about?

Quite apart from providing solicitors with a rich pas-ture – an Elysium Fields of profitable litigation – shar-ing can really work, assuming that the participants are civilised human beings[1]. All that is required is a degree of compatibility. Ideally the couples involved should be:

- Two Yachtmasters with hairy tufts in their ears mar-ried to two wives of impeccable tidiness who sleep with a J-cloth in one hand and a bottle of Mister Sheen in the other, or

- Two total muffins married to two total slatterns.

The crux of the matter is the state in which the boat is left. The following little exchange may serve to illustrate the problem.

Wife: 'Well you saw how I left the boat, Gerald. You could have eaten out of my sink and my toilet bowl was a picture, a picture I tell you! The boat was a little palace. Look at it now. I could WEEP, Gerald . . . GERALD!'

Gerald: 'Ummm dear?'

The inventory

A fictional list of equipment so-called because it is 'invented' by an owner for the purpose of selling the boat. The novice, greatly impressed, may pore over this lengthy document with excitement. 'I see she's got no

---

[1] Capable of any sort of mayhem.

fewer than twenty pin-less shackles and ten shackle-less pins!' he enthuses, wondering what the hell they are.

The inventory offers a tally of teaspoons (various), crockery, pots and pans. The vendor's wife will have done a bit of swapping. 'They're not getting my good pan!' she snarls, substituting one that has never been the same since she tried that jam recipe. She adds a torn plastic apron to ease her conscience.

The same policy is applied to fenders and warps, the former substitution being flat as a bachelor's omelette, and the later, worn-out halyards end-for-ended more times than boarding house sheets.

A wise buyer will wish to examine the sails, and if the boat is laid up this may mean a visit to the vendor's home and the boy's bedroom. Bags will be produced from under the bed (along with several regrettable magazines) and a cautious few inches of each sail pulled out for inspection. It is not unreasonable to ask to see the whole sail. Mainsail, headsails, spinnaker and storm jib soon fill the room with billowing folds plus the crackling resentment of the vendor. As you take your departure it is courteous to promise that you will be 'letting him know . . .' This little gesture will be appreciated.

Instruments will be produced, still warm from the airing cupboard, indicating either commendable care or that they have just been whisked home in a hurry, dripping condensation and growing the sort of mould culture associated with experiments in cloning and the prospect of four-legged hens. The vendor will swear to their accuracy and narrate feats of navigation undertaken with their aid that make the exploits of Magellan sound like a pedalo on a park lake.

Safety equipment

It is wiser to buy it brand new. The inventory may include six lifejackets which subside like the death of fairy Tinkerbell ten minutes after inflation, and two dry-powder fire extinguishers which sound like a Cuban Band when shaken. The red flares were time-expired at about the time of Mafeking and there is a liferaft, oval from being sat on, which offers about as much guarantee of salvation as Lucky Joan the Wad.

When buying a new liferaft, it is important to know how much of a tug is required to trigger off inflation and conversely how *small* a tug can be safely given in the course of normal handling. Ask the salesman to demonstrate. Stand well to the rear just in case he is new to his job.

The same thing applies to pyrotechnics; how little/much of a tug is required to discharge the signal? A parachute flare or three-star red belting round and round the saloon can undermine your authority. Ask for a safe demonstration. Do not be afraid to take your custom elsewhere.

Chapter Two

Learning the art

There are methods of learning
For the discerning
Which are meant to improve-us
Like when we knocks
Chunks off docks.
This is known as 'manoeuvres'.

As this modest work is dedicated to 'family cruising', it would have been helpful if we had been able to monitor the progress of a typical family of cruising novices. Since the prospect of a subsequent bumpy journey through the Libel Courts whipped the smile off the Publisher's face like an Undertaker's catalogue, the author has been forced to invent such a family. Meet the Trouts:

Gerald Trout, Father. An oil executive[1], he carries that firm on his back and lets them walk all over him! Known afloat as 'father' or the Master Under God (the MUG).

Miriam Trout, Mother/mate/cook/prophet, who said the above. Yoga class Wednesday mornings.

Sandra Trout, daughter aged 13. Would rather be mucking out stables and it's not *fair*, so there!

Norris Trout, son. Boy Scout aged 12. Leader of Whimbrel patrol. Life dedicated to finding a use for the sheepshank. To be known as The Boy.

[1] A sardine wholesaler.

Bosco, Wife's brother. About as much use on deck as a wheelbarrow in a dark alley. Knows quite a lot about the life-cycle of the warble-fly.

First steps

We will assume that father at least has learned the rudiments of dinghy sailing, perhaps on a council Adult Education course.

He is the richer for a certificate of (limited) Competence and the poorer by fifty quid – two days of shuddering under the resigned eye of an instructor who has suffered more dippings than a Cheviot ram.

Lifejacketed students in groups of four, and looking like poached eggs, took it in turns to hold the tiller on, off and dead into the wind. Spectators gathered and waited patiently for lesson number two: How to Gybe.

'Awww!' they winced delightedly.

The instructor nerved himself for the inevitable. 'Get ready to shift your weight, Mrs Prendergast. No, I am *not* being offensive. Helm up slowly . . . SLOWLY! No, I am *not* shouting, Mrs Prendergast. Ah. AH NO . . . Well just tread water, Mrs Prendergast, and let go of my hair please!'

For the price of a skinned shin and a lump on his head like a doorbell, father leaves the course bursting with vital knowledge and eager to pass it on to his little crew. He tells them of the treats in store. 'I was *not* rolling my eyes,' says mother, 'I was merely inspecting the ceiling for cobwebs.'

Evening classes

It is strongly recommended that skipper and mate should attend jointly. Most boroughs provide a wealth of Adult Education evening classes ranging from Creative Dance, Sugarcraft and Practical Composting to Quilting and Lipreading – the latter being of special value in cockpit cocktail parties, eg 'Don't open another bottle, Gerald, or they'll never go!'

Be prepared to sit on plastic chairs of unparalleled discomfort for two hours, by which time the entire class will be performing a sort of sitting Cossack dance in its quest for a more comfortable position.

You will be taught that there is no law against taking a fix by a teacher possessing such a weather-beaten complexion that, coupled with narrowed horizon-scanning eyes, it is like being addressed by a letterbox. He will also teach you how to apply your Variation[2].

Cruising courses

These can offer an excellent grounding[3]. Unhappily they can have a sorry effect upon the morale. The student of modest aptitude will come up against a fellow-student called (by instructors) Well-done-Jack (or Tom, Shane, Bertha etc). Repeatedly our student of modest talents will have to listen to cries of, 'You've-got-it-Jane', 'Nice-one-Tom' and so on. This has the effect of making a right muffin of our less-able pupils who at once, and without hesitation, put a foot through a skylight, catch a riding turn or drop the boom, driving the instructor's cap down over his ears like the lid of a pickle jar.

Versions of Well-done-Jack vary from a man with a prominent Adam's apple and a rucksack which is apparently glued to his back like the shell of a snail and Hilda from Surbiton who wears navy culottes and says 'Good-O'. In their most hated form, they are aged about eleven and wear baseball caps back-to-front.

They master the-going-alongside-under-engine exercise at once and it is 'Bang-on Jack/Hilda!' 'Nice one . . . You've got it' etc. Our less adept student attempts it and leaves the instructor white-faced and struggling to regain the powers of speech.

[2] Nightly and massaged well in.
[3] You'll be doing a lot of that.

In the navigation period, our paragon will have completed his/her set problem and be wandering around looking out of windows while our muffin is still nursing the belief that LAT is some sort of toilet facility. All of which combines to reduce the moderately self-possessed to a state of nervous uncertainty and the timid to a craven jelly – a prime target for Welfare Counselling.

Here we go then

Let us assume then that our little band of 'laughing fellow rovers' have acquired their boat, twenty-six feet of fun-afloat, a 5/6 berth sloop with diesel aux, sal dintte with fttd matrsses and fll invnty. They bought her afloat in the marina scndhnd only 1 ownr. They have no fears as to the integrity of the vendor who is a Special Constable and whose brother-in-law's father is a Member of Parliament. He very kindly found a surveyor for them who will carry out a survey at a special rate.

So here we are aboard. Ahoy there, time to go to sea! But first of all we must listen to a shipping forecast. This doom-laden narrative covers the whole of the British Isles but we only want our own little bit. This means that we must all keep quiet and concentrate hard. Concentrating on *concentrating* will inevitably mean that we will miss it or perhaps hear 'Yoo-hoo!' – it's the Wilkins who have come to see us off – or at the critical moment, the toilet overflows.

Useless though all this may seem, it does give father (Master Under God or the MUG) an opportunity to sit with pursed lips, frowning at the plate rack with pencil poised and bellowing for silence.

Before venturing out to sea, let us review our safety drills, eg fire extinguisher and red flares.

Note: The Boy may offer his services but *do not* let him get his grubby little mitts on them, or the former is likely to be needed for extinguishing the latter.

A valuable simulated liferaft drill can be carried out while alongside in the marina by substituting a saloon settee mattress for the raft. At the cry 'Abandon ship!' hurl a mattress on to the catwalk, don lifejackets, and to a cry of ONE, TWO, etc leap upon it and crouch there while going through the motions of paddling. Father will simulate the sending of a MAYDAY call by pinching his nostrils while speaking through the cardboard tube from a toilet roll. This will lend his tone a certain 'timbre'. 'MAYDAY MAYDAY MAYDAY, yacht LITTLE PIPIT LITTLE PIPIT LITTLE PIPIT I spell Papa-India-Papa' etc.

Note: Do not be surprised to find that a small group of spectators has gathered. Photos may be taken.

The occupants of nearby moored yachts may join in by dragging the mattress and its riders up and down the catwalk while simulating the sound of wind and water, ships, sirens etc. This is helpful.

There is one final precaution to be taken before 'casting off'. The Coastguard must be informed of our departure. Be concise but informative. Let go all ropes and proceed as follows:

SO-AND-SO COASTGUARD (3 times) YACHT LITTLE PIPIT (3 times) 'We're going for a little sail. There's us and the wife's brother from Skegness OVER.'

The Coastguard, being stuck in an old office all day, will be eager to hear this detailed plan and about the cold drumsticks which were on Special Offer.

Out to sea

A beginner in a yacht marina sticks out like a baseball cap in the Ascot Royal Enclosure. The crews of adjoining yachts will eagerly view the novice's departure with the ghoulish anticipation of a Roman audience watching the entry of the Christians. It therefore behoves our family of novices to proceed with circumspection.

By now father should have perfected The Voice of Authority. This is a tone of sleepy boredom akin to that of a sales-girl at a perfumery counter when asked what she's got for under a fiver. The crew should respond by drawing down the corners of their mouths, yawning and rolling their eyes. With hands to stations we are ready to go. Bosco is forward, The Boy is aft, Sandra is painting her toenails in the forepeak and Mum, with uncanny foresight, stays the hell out of it and polishes the loo as if it was going to be presented at Court.

With the engine running flat out astern and warps humming like bees in some bosky dell, our small barky seems eager to be off. Father raises a moistened finger. The crews of nearby yachts have gathered in their cockpits where they jockey for a clear view. Some have invited guests; cool drinks are served; small bets are exchanged, and thumbs are poised on the buttons of camcorders. Father clears his throat . . .

'Eggowaft,' he drawls to The Boy.

'Organaft,' pipes the lad, letting go aft.

Up forward Bosco is examining the mast for signs of warble-fly.

'Eggoford,' drones father sleepily, trying to hide the tremolo in his voice.

'Organford,' murmurs Bosco, hurling the entire rope overboard followed by two fenders and the windlass handle.

The yacht exits from her berth as if propelled by some vast and unloving boot. The audience, on its feet, cheers raggedly. Out in the open our yacht must now be turned 180° to head seaward. The diagrams on page 23 will explain how this should be done. If the wind is blowing *out* of the berth her stern will immediately cock to the left (or maybe right) calling for full right (or maybe left) rudder. Neither will make the slightest difference.

By now father will be alone on deck, Bosco and Boy having read the runes and decided to get the hell below and pretend to dip the sump. Rendered dumb by reason of his tongue being stuck to the roof of his mouth (there may also be froth), father proceeds to work the tiller and gear lever as if practising the stick dance. Bells at his knees and ribbons on his hat is all that is needed to complete the spectacle.

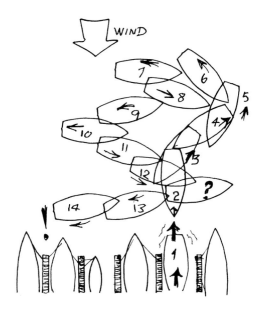

The yacht drifts bodily sideways to bring up athwart the bows of yachts berthed opposite where he is welcomed by a solid frieze of jabbing boathooks and thrusting fenders. By listening attentively, he will be able to pick up many valuable nuggets of advice regarding his technique, recommended destination and parentage.

Should the wind have been blowing *into* the berth, however, there will be a bigger crash and the yacht will be plastered across the bows of adjoining boats like a jam flan on a diner's elbow. Father may not be altogether sure of his ability to put his tiller where advised by the heavy-breathing man with the milk and cornflakes in his hair. Having extricated his command from either of these situations and with spectators waving God-speed and blunt instruments, our Master Under God (MUG) turns his brave bows seaward at last.

If our marina happens to be situated in a ferry port the best time to leave is just as this vessel is approaching the harbour entrance as other traffic will be minimal at that time. He will not be surprised at hearing the ferry give a cheerful toot or several on her siren. He should return this comradely signal with a toot upon his own horn. (Lacking such, a cardboard party kazoo or cracker trumpet is a good substitute). 'Yippee!' he may cry, blowing it and waving. He may be rewarded by seeing the ferry captain in person come to the wing of his bridge and make gestures.

In passing, let us note that one should never go alongside in the ferry berth when she is absent. You may not expect to be very long but should she return without warning you are likely to end up very, very long and very, very narrow.

Under sail

As our little vessel heads seawards through the harbour entrance our hearts, like the toilet bowl, may be brimming over. Head-to-wind she bounces, curtseys, slams and rolls, a motion which flushes out those still below like a sulphur candle down a rat-hole. 'All hands to make sail!' cries the skipper.

Each has his or her appointed place, Bosco staggering forward to his jib halyard, The Boy, with his scoutly accoutrements flashing, makes for the main halyard. Mum, being nobody's fool, holds on to a limp rope's end while Sandra, on the settee, wrestles with drying her nails.

'Hoist yer main and let go yer topping lift,' cries father stirringly.

'Let go me topping lift and hoist me main,' echoes the lad doing so.

There is a loud BOOM (which is how that spar gets its name) and father slumps to his knees with eyes crossed and tongue lolling.

Meanwhile Bosco, receiving no orders, uses his initiative (it is the only one he's got). An extractor fan and a stamp collection make a better combination than Bosco and his initiative.

Up goes the jib all aback and around we spin, boom threshing about like Drake laying waste to Cadiz. Father slumps back to his knees with crossed eyes and lolling tongue and the slashing mainsheet triggers off the yellow smoke canister.

Ashore, a vigilant Coastguard has levelled his binoculars. He dials the Lifeboat House. 'I ah have ah yellow smoke bearing ah Wun-ah, nine-ah, fifeah,' he intones. The lifeboat Coxswain is in the middle of watching the big fight on telly and he finds the news emotionally disturbing, as does the boot-assisted cat.

One hour and a lot of cringing and fat contribution later, our small ship is heeling to the wind as she humps, lurches, bangs and screws her way to windward

with a bone in her teeth. Father's teeth are in his pocket. He moistens a finger and holds it aloft.

A trawler load of fishermen with huge fists and hard-boiled red faces is passing. He is careful to raise only one finger.

'By Harry this is the stuff to give 'em'. He groans, following tradition. He blows his cheeks out and eructates *sotto voce* (there are clinics where this can be treated confidentially). With a shudder, he eyes the ranked and upturned buttocks of his crew at the lee rail. 'Grit your teeth, chaps,' he advises, evoking images of frosty roads and Council lorries, too late as usual. It is advice wasted on Bosco who has also goff them in iff poffet.

Steering

A novice may feel a little disconcerted at being asked to 'do a trick at the helm'. Nothing elaborate is called for however, perhaps something simple such as holding a pencil between upper lip and nose or singing a verse of the Marseillaise while drinking a cup of water will suffice – both are old favourites and certain to win a smile.

Steering, on the other hand, is a serious art and not easy to grasp (as the man with the ferret down his breeks laughingly asserted). Teenagers however, well accustomed to video games in which contestants zap one another and fall down ladders, can steer a straight course unerringly, in some cases for as long as one minute at a time if their attention is not distracted.

Compass steering   Watching the compass is like following the flight of the butterfly on its quest for nectar, a swoop, a pause, another swoop, and on and on while the tiller is heaved this way and that mimicking the swipes of the lepidopterist's net as he blunders after his colourful prey.

Having once married course to lubberline a steersman or woman is said to be 'in the groove': a trance-like state not to be disturbed. Accordingly voices are lowered and no sudden movements are made in the vicinity of the helm. It is like being in a public library, an aura of sibilant hissing conversations and disapproving bifocals.

Like the holy anchorite in his gloomy cave, contemplating a skull as if waiting for it to play a tune and denied all nourishment, our steersperson must not be distracted by food.

While the rest of the crew sit slurping from pint mugs and chomping their ginger nuts our subject is on the astral plane and steering with utter dedication. Then the navigator has to spoil it by sticking his great hooter in. 'What are you making?' he honks.

An experienced person would know the right answer. 'I'm averaging XXX (the course),' he/she might drawl, lying through his/her teeth in a tone of thinly-veiled dislike.

Our novice, bobble-cap a'bobbin', has no such artifice. 'Oh,' might come the faltering reply, 'Oh, nothing at the moment but I'm quite keen on fretwork.'

The navigator – and God knows he's a patient man – rolls his eyes upwards seeking calm. 'I mean your course, your *head,* man. Can't you hold it?'

Our tyro lets go of the tiller and clutches his great daft poll. Howls rend the air. Thereafter he steers as if he were icing a cake with a leaky bag.

Steering by the wind A reach or a dead run might be ordered or perhaps a *closehauled leg* all irrespective of a compass heading.

For the novice this can mean total confusion. The command to 'run off' may invite our tyro to do so, taking the tiller with him/her. Also, and in a mixed sex crew, the order to 'see if you can reach her' or 'pinch her up a bit' can lead to unsolicited familiarity, a ringing belt around the earhole and that's enough of that thank you very much.

Tacking and gybing The command 'Ready to go about' (eg with Mike Tyson or Frank Bruno for example) is a jocular reference to the good hiding received during the former manoeuvre. 'My helm is DOWN. Lee Ho!' cries the helmsman whereupon the world as we know it today dissolves into a bedlam of lashing ropes, swiping spars and thunderous noise. The crew cowers and father sinks to his knees with crossed eyes and lolling tongue.

If the helmsman continues to hold the helm down the fracas will die away quickly and a great peace will reign, the wind will fall to a zephyr and the air becomes warm, calm and pleasant as the boat heaves herself upright. Crew's heads emerge from hoods and peer around warily. Then the Flying Scot comes out of the tunnel. There is a tremendous CRASH. The crew cowers and father sinks to his knees, etc etc.

The yacht has both tacked *and* gybed but no harm has been done that a spot of therapy on a hard couch cannot remedy by turning it into a recollection of childhood trauma.

We have learned much, and in particular that the only truly safe place to be when aboard a boat under sail is adopting the foetal position in the forepeak, hands clasped behind neck and reciting the Apostles' Creed in a strong voice.

Winches The protuberances sticking up on the cockpit coamings are not, as might be supposed, for the purpose of draining wellies or cracking crab claws, they are for winding ropes around. Ten or twelve turns are quite enough and there is no need to wrap the whole sheet around it each time. This is known as 'taking a turn'. Thus the command 'Take a turn there!' should not evoke the reply that you have just had a turn and that somebody else ought to have a go. This would be showing Bad Grace. Let her find out for herself.

Triangular courses Each member of the crew should take his/her turn to act as skipper sailing the boat on a tight triangular course of run, reach and closehauled leg. For this a windward mark is needed, preferably this will be a navigation buoy – perhaps marking some hazard and therefore shunned by all other traffic.

Alternatively a solitary angler in his anchored dinghy makes a good substitute. Each helmsperson should endeavour to round the 'mark' as closely as possible. Remember a polite 'Good day' to the angler costs nothing.

Should the angler suddenly be seen to jerk around and begin to follow in hot pursuit this may indicate that his tackle is foul of your rudder. A bread knife lashed to the boathook will effect his release quickly and win you his cheery wave of gratitude.

As in all things though, fair play is essential. Wait until he is once more firmly anchored and settled to his fishing before resuming your circuits.

Re-berthing the yacht

As the reader who has persisted thus far with this modest work will realise, and as our imaginary Trout family will have demonstrated, there are unsuspected obstacles ahead. No pantomime Lucifer bursting upwards through the stage floor with a chilling cry of 'HO-HO!' and encountering a faulty trapdoor can ever be so thwarted as the novice yachtsman faced with a complex manoeuvre and aided by a crew of total muffins.

We have navigated out of our marina berth, forged seawards and carried out a series of beneficial exercises and now it is time to return to our berth – just as the balloonist must return to earth and the bird to its twig.

Our novice is in a similar situation to the airline passenger – the only person on board who *didn't* have the prawn curry – who is now faced with the problems of a talk-down landing. 'You say you are presently located *under* the pilot's seat,' says the Ground-Controller heavily, aware of the long and harrowing dialogue ahead. He gulps. 'Now, shall we begin by opening our eyes, sir . . .'

It is to be hoped that conditions are quiet, that the calm of Elysium Fields pertains, where hidden flutes fill the still air with liquid magic and gossamer-winged fairies hover o'er limpid waters, when father makes his first attempt to re-enter his berth or he may otherwise be doomed to create the spectacle of the week. The motives of solo round-the-world yachtsmen take on a new meaning. They are scared to face berthing.

There is always the option of delegation. Father eyes Bosco with crafty intent. He waits until the easy bit is done and the marina lies ahead. He gives a laugh and claps hand to head.

'There, look at me hogging the helm! Here,' he invites. 'Here, somebody else have a go. Bosco?'

Father has the conscience of an Arms Baron and he knows the scope of Bosco's chequebook.

Singlemindedness is what it's about. The inexperienced mountaineer following the straining lederhosen of his Tyrolean Guide up some perilous and precipice-flanked ledge eyes the jerking leather rump fixedly. 'A fine panorama ya!' prompts this expert stopping without warning. There is silence . . . followed by a far, thin wail.

Stopping is going to be our problem and the crew should have been well rehearsed in the art of heaving a line to some well-wisher (hopefully) ashore and ready to take it.

The thrower must establish him/herself as being the person in charge although it is possible for a situation to develop where there are *two* nellies – one ashore and one on board – in which case there are several likely alternative situations possible.

1 Both make fast their ends of the rope and stand back with pride.
2 Both let go at the same time.
3 Both pull in slack vigorously. There is a loud splash.

As soon as our little ship appears and begins heading for the marina, crews of yachts moored in adjacent berths begin massing and murmuring. 'It looks like trouble at t'mill, lad. The men are looking ugly, son.'

Father, with the end now in sight, like some far-faring mariner with bananas in his rigging and toredo up his tuck, senses a welcoming committee and raises a hand self-deprecatingly.

It was nothing, he implies, anyone could have done the same. Which is where he is wrong. Nobody, no one, could make such a howling cock-up as he is about to achieve.

Stopping is the crux of the problem and merely ramming the engine full astern is not the solution. Banging an engine from full ahead to full astern can have it spitting teeth like a barefist boxer. The second method of stopping which involves Bosco sitting in the bows with his boots stuck out is about as much use as the wagging finger of King Canute as a means of stemming the advancing tide.

On the other hand, judicious use of gear levers and throttle (often and disastrously one and the same control) can achieve much. However, as any church hall juggler will affirm, it's all right as long as you don't *think* about what your hands are doing.

Father is faced with a dilemma, also a hulking great baulk of timber supporting the catwalk, whereon there stands an excited groups of hell-wishers urging him onwards. His nerveless hand finds the lever which is in neutral . . . he rams it full astern . . . voices howl encouragement and advice . . . he rams it full ahead. Our frail barky drives shudderingly up and onto the catwalk. It is like striking the *Lutine* bell at Lloyd's. The air is filled with the sound of sobbing Names and pounding Docksiders. Sirens scream as an ambulance full of Counsellors arrives on the scene. The Trouts are back.

Chapter Three

Why not charter?

There's a special rate, booking early or late
In what they call the 'low season'.
The Autumn's unruly and blowing a hooley,
And in Springtime it's bloody near freezin'.

There can be few more dismal sights than the new owner pounding up and down in driving rain, newly aware of a leak in the seat of his oily pants and conscious of the marina bill awaiting payment when he gets back.

Experienced sailors balance the delights of ownership against such minor tribulations and remain firm in their convictions. It is all worthwhile. How can our tyro, wide-eyed as Little Dolly Dimples, be expected to know whether ownership is going to be enjoyable? How can one taste before buying? The answer lies in the *charter boat holiday*.

Such a holiday can range from bare-boat (nothing in it) charter in a canal barge with the overall speed of a Galapagos tortoise and a different mooring every night two miles from the previous one, to an outright Mediterranean charter with skipper and crew thrown in[1]. There is also the group Flotilla Cruise wherein a dozen identical yachts blunder after a Leader from port-to-port and

[1] It has been known.

anchorage-to-anchorage, in a sort of cross between an 'O'Grady Says' game and an Easter pilgrimage. Or, with experience, one might either sail unchaperoned (and hopefully unobserved) or as a paying crew.

The permanent skipper

When the arrangement includes a permanent skipper (and possibly crew) we must begin by understanding the relationship of client to skipper. The rookie who pays a drill sergeant to chase him around the barrack square, howling vituperation at his inadequacy, is in similar guise to the novice/skipper relationship while entering a lock with a following wind and a duff engine. Finally, bruised and battered, sporting flattened finger tips, spectacles repaired with Sellotape and Musto oilies ripped up the back as if they'd been filleted, they scribble their cheques with touching gratitude for a marvellous time and vow to come again.

The paying crew

There is an ocean of difference between your old time cloth cap and trouser clip lodger, who likes a nice bit o' liver for his tea, and your paying guest (PG). We're into a bit of quality with your PG, Mahler in the parlour and an en suite bedroom. None of your bumping around at 2 am after the darts match, looking for the loo and a distressing dénouement involving the linen cupboard. Lodger and PG share the owner's marmalade, loo roll and *Daily Mirror*.

It must always be remembered that the yacht is being run as a means of transferring money from your wallet to that of the owner. It may be a man/wife team. He has sunk his gratuity in it – an adventure smacking of distress rockets and blanket-shrouded figures in a lifeboat. It is probably making a whacking great loss. He is most likely to be one of those luckless people who take the last seat in the bus without checking who's in the one next to him. 'Good morning. I say, what luck, eh!'

'Bordig,' sneezes his snuffling neighbour.

Let us take a closer look at the life of the paying-crew holiday yacht and its man/wife team. The owner-skipper-navigator-engineer and general big-head aided by his wife-mate-cook-secretary-hostess and casual skivvy. We find them taking their ease following the departure of one lot and prior to the arrival of the next. 'You must make more effort to be pleasant at breakfast' she tells him.

He is not a morning man. He reads the cornflake packet in numbing silence as if absorbed in the plot. A Parish Council Meeting might be a barrel of laughs by comparison. Next time he will try a *joke*.

Worse yet is the Oh-what-a-beautiful-morning man, the hand-rubbing Let's-get-the-show-on-the-road man, overjoyed to know that everybody slept well, the Call-me-Tony metaphorically Kick-the-cat man. This show of camaraderie is about as substantial as paper knickers in a downpour.

The mate shades her eyes. 'I think that's *them*!' she raps tersely. 'You'd better look!' He uses the binoculars. 'Oh my God!' he breathes, crossing himself. 'He's wearing a bloody yachting cap!'

Their faces work with emotion. This is an omen of disaster comparable to the ghostly piper O'Glen-some-thing-or-other. A yachting cap implies some knowledge of yachting. Its wearer may *offer opinions*. He may even want to *navigate*. 'Dear Lord, not the running fix again . . . !'

Gradually he relaxes. It is a crackling brand new yachting cap and doubtless there will be a SUPA-BI VALUE sticker on it. Experience tells him that here is a right narna, ready to open his beak with gratitude for any nautical albeit fictional worm that may be fed to him. It betokens an easy cruise and lots of time in harbour to catch up on the varnishing.

His relief is short-lived. There appears a lad in trainers so vast that he appears to be standing on a pedestal. He has ears like a test-your-grip machine, he stands about seven feet tall and is six inches thick. *He carries a fishing rod!* With Divine Grace he will not be a Proper Angler and demanding trolling speed, rocks and room in the fridge for his ragworms. If he is the usual run of mackerel-killer, vows the skipper, they shall eat every last goddam one he catches!

The skipper now finds something inscrutable to do to the engine, leaving confrontation to his mate . . .

'Welcome aboard,' she oils, switching it on like a bed-side lamp. 'This is the skipper,' she introduces, giving his buttocks a hard eye. He emerges, wearing his smile like a clip-on bow tie – and like that ornament it can become detached and left swinging by one claw with very little provocation.

On deck, all stand in an uncertain group, bumping into one another in the way of total beginners newly aboard a boat. 'Shall we go below then?' the mate invites, leading the way. They follow, heads rhythmically clouting the deckbeam like a bamboo zylophone. In the saloon they seem to take up more room than a detachment of Guards in busbies and full marching order.

There will be a skipper's briefing which is brief indeed. It covers use of fresh water, booze and loos. There is a

kitty for the drink. Nobody will *dare* to wash or use the john for fear of blocking it.

Then for the benefit of the ladies the mate-cook-hostess provides some extra and more specific instruction in the complexity of knobs, handles and valves which constitute a mechanical toilet. They learn that it is inadvisable to attempt usage while bucketing to windward and *never* on starboard tack. The whole operation is like being required to start up and then sit astride a lawnmower but never to empty your grass-box in harbour.

While the outright charterer has some say in where the yacht goes the paying crew goes wherever the skipper decides. They have worn tramlines between Solent, Cherbourg and Guernsey.

He has a repertoire of ploys aimed at extra days in port for the purpose of patching up the boat. 'So we won't be sailing today?' hazards a little man whose nose is painted white with sunblock like some species of ornamental fowl. The skipper glances at the sky and shakes his head. It is an unbroken blue but it is *the wrong sort of blue*. He has also taken the secret precaution of readjusting the barometer to read a chilling 960 mbs.

Relationships can go a bit sour. Everybody is invited to share all chores including the steering – which is a likely source of friction when the skipper is navigating and lost. If only people would steer the course ordered for-God's-sake!

Up on deck the helm as usual is the social centre. Everybody is being anecdotal over coffee and Thin Rich Tea biscuits. The ship's wake looks like a barograph reading off SE Iceland. He rears up out of companionway.

'Can we just watch our steering please,' he pipes in his surely-not-too-much-to-ask voice. 'We're not on the dodgems now!'

The silence which follows this little outburst marks the opening of the gulf between Them and Them.

Henceforth the paying crew begin a whispering exchange of the latest examples of owner-villainy and parsimonious behaviour regarding butter. The owner and his wife swap the latest anecdotes featuring the howling stupidity of their guests. 'Do come again,' they coo waving goodbye with the cheque. Oh they will . . . they will.

The outright charter

The outright charterer becomes a short-time owner with the paid skipper and crew to do his bidding. Thereafter he has only to say where he wants to go and Hey Presto the skipper comes up with three well-rehearsed reasons why this is totally out of the question.

Supine charterers are willing to be trundled around the circuit like meals-on-wheels – luke-warm custard and no onions for *Mon Repose*. They will be told where the best shell-encrusted souvenirs can be bought, where to eat and where to buy curiously-expensive wine – all recommendations carrying remunerative cheer for the skipper. Alternatively they can prove to be antagonistic, obdurate and unwilling to be pushed around by any jumped-up fink in a comic hat.

This is financial disaster for the paid help. The charterer, so it seems, hasn't paid good money just to sit around in harbour. His aim is to see how many ports can be crammed into the minimum number of days and if ever the engine gets cold somebody isn't trying.

The charterer and his party eat ashore when expected aboard and demand a meal aboard having said they'll be going ashore to dine. In the galley the atmosphere grows critical and lips are stretched thinner than jam on a boarding house butty. The meal will be corned beef hash or lump-it.

The full charter may mean bimini-tops and West Indian coral sand, a fridge hammering away day and night to humour the American preoccupation for having a frozen palate and locals flogging conches to honkies. It can also mean the Mediterranean where wealthy people charter monolithic yachts just in order to have their nubile daughters pursued around the sundeck by panting stewards.

Full charter in home waters is altogether rarer – perhaps a venture to the Western Isles of Scotland where there will be bagpipes, scenery, double-knit sweaters and midges the size of Harrier Jump Jets.

Bareboat charter

The more experienced charterer may prefer to sail unaided by owner or paid help. Written evidence is required to show that he/she is the safest and most experienced navigator since Captain Cook. This means letters wrung out of a yacht club Commodore on the usual go-on-have-another basis. There is then a wide choice of yachts available.

The initial take-over should include a detailed examination of everything aboard from the settee stuffing to the state of the owner's bunions. In fact it is more likely to mean a rapid tour of the electrics and plumbing given by the owner and a rhythmic nodding of the head by the charterer.

Later it will appear that the warps are both few and disgraceful, that there is a total absence of stuff for lashing things and barely sufficient assorted tools (tls asstd) to open a jar of jam, and that the salt is moist.

The handing back at the end of an event-packed cruise is as brief as the charterer can make it and it gives a whole new meaning to the expression 'spit-and-polish'. The scarred varnishwork being temporarily remedied by the one and the chip out of the toerail (an anchoring emergency) by the other.

Bareboat charters range from canal and (leaking) 'character' craft to the overseas boat owned by an Austrian in Italy and equipped with French charts and a German pilotbook.

The flotilla

For the novice family the Flotilla holiday is an outing with nanny and it has almost everything to recommend it. Let us therefore watch our fictional family as they arrive at some distant airport where the temperature is Gas Mark Six. They are welcomed by dusty policemen festooned with weapons and a flotilla agent waving a cereal packet. It is the wrong way round. The other side says SUNSOAK FLOTLER in felt-tip.

They will join a fleet of perhaps a dozen identical yachts moored amongst dead cats in a picturesque setting of Coca Cola ads and burger bars. Fellow crews vary in competence, the more faded their sailing wear the more advanced their experience and our adventurers eye with respect the toe-blasted deck shoes and tattered knee-caps. How thankful they are for their own carefully violated garments.

There is a family of howling novices fresh from a crasher dinghy course who contemplate sailing hour with the enthusiasm of condemned men eyeing sunrise and there is The-Man-Who-Has-Been-Before, self-nominated expert on all that lies ahead. Stick-by-him, he says, and you'll be OK.

The leader yacht is crewed by The Flotilla Leader, usually Antipodean and in this case a New Zealander who will refer confusingly to 'litting go the inker'. There is the engineer who will tackle anything from a scavenge pump to a pacemaker and the hostess. She wears shorts so tight that she walks on tip-toe and advises on hygiene, provisioning and gives the ladies a good old whispering-to about 'certain matters'.

There is a daily Skippers Briefing, usually an all-male cabal held over coffee at which skippers scribble illegible notes about incomprehensible manoeuvres. They are reminded not to carry too much hidway when coming to inker and not to get ahid of the leader yacht.

The Man-Who-Has-Been-Before sits yawning and admiring the scenery. He has even brought his own chart. He will ask a question in order to show that he already knows the answer. 'Am I right in supposing that so-and-so is such-and-such?' He will sail ahead of the leader throughout and the leader mentally vows to git this bistid before he's done.

The Flotilla Leader is revered by the noddies as a cross between Lord Nelson and Kevin Keegan. He wears miniscule shorts of tattered denim filled to bursting point by muscular thighs the colour of a Regency sideboard.

Father hasn't worn shorts since that week in Marbella, now rendered memorable by the baggage handlers' strike and a dodgy paella. He goes below to change. 'You're going to put them on then,' says lady-wife in flat tones. Any confidence he may have had evaporates like spit on a hot stove.

Up on deck he goes. Brand new navy knickers, mid-calf length and knife-edged. He wears his ordinary socks pulled well up – they have this zig-zag pattern. His legs have the livid, luminous whiteness of well blanched celery. Bystanders glance aside out of common decency as at some dreadful disfigurement deserving of compassion and tact.

The programme consists of day sails but includes a 'free cruising period' for the adventurous which allows holidaymakers an opportunity to be fleeced rotten by carpet salesmen. All except The Man-Who etc who sails in the opposite direction to everybody else. He is the subject of heated phone calls between Embassy and Turkish (Greek, Italian etc) Naval Intelligence.

There will be the barbecue with garlic bread and strangely alien-looking sausages containing something unidentifiable and ominously chewy. A beach campfire of fireproof driftwood produces billowing clouds of smoke through which guests grope and peer with streaming eyes like the souls of the damned.

Jolly communal meals ashore will be eaten in picturesque palm-thatched hovels, where the chance of even the most basic form of kitchen hygiene is about as likely as encountering a top-hatted doorman with an umbrella. Sandra breaks a fingernail. There is a 'genuine' *bouillabaisse*. 'You won't get one like this in Soho!' sneers father. It is like looking down an open manhole. It looks like a job for Dyna-Rod. Camcorders preserve for a yawning posterity innumerable toasts drunk in the sort of red wine that combats rust and penetrates seized threads.

The final communal meal of the holiday, following the 'race' and the best-kept-yacht competition (a shameless ploy to get people to clean up their own mess), is enlivened by gypsy dancing. All join in, forming a long line. This is a timely rehearsal for the flight home next day and an unbroken queue for the loos.

Two particular features dominate the cruise, the 'holding tank' and berthing bows-to. Later, people will meet up and recall them as old shellbacks might recall rounding Cape Horn or a typhoon off Taiwan.

In the interests of the environment, holding tanks aboard boats constitute a permanent quag of unspeakable foulness, added to constantly in harbour and at intervals taken to sea and *pumped out* to the great delight of seabirds and to the revulsion of anybody astern. Holding tanks are never quite big enough. With a full crew (to take advantage of price concessions), two days in dock and you're about to go critical, the overflow is reaching its revolting and bubbling limitations. Usage becomes rationed. The alternative is a two hundred yard sprint along echoing pontoons to the public conveniences – you will dine out on your account of what you found . . . with the price of failure beyond contemplation.

Anchoring bows-to is one of the greatest of all threats to marital harmony. The theory is that you approach the quay head-on, letting go a stern anchor at exactly the right moment so that you end up with your bows mere inches short of the stonework, an easy step ashore. The brutal truth is that you either hit it such a clout that the town hall clock starts chiming or you bring up three feet short. Tight jeans and a three foot gap equate with tantrums. Father, ashore, reaches out a hand. 'Give me your hand, dear, and you'll be fine!' he lies desperately. That blows it.

Does he really think she's going to make an exhibition of herself? Well, *does* he? 'Oh go ahead. Leave me. *I'm quite happy.*' So was Robinson Crusoe.

It'll be the package to Lanzarote next year and that's final.

Chapter Four

Joining a club

AGMs mean elections, low in the affections
Of those who don't want to be chosen.
They crouch low in their seats
Heads-between-feets
Hoping no one will propose 'em.

When you join a club you become part of a great family. It is like inviting all your relations to stay over Christmas. The novice will be welcomed with open arms (palms in the case of lovable old Ned the boatman) and introduced to all by the club secretary. 'Here is our new member,' he will proclaim. 'Oh really,' members will reply lowering their muzzles back into their pints.

It is not wise for a novice to betray his ignorance. All the other novices will instantly shower him with advice, thereby chucking off the mantle of club patsy from their own shoulders and awarding this ignomy to him as in a game of tag or 'you're it'.

Novice status must be kept a dark secret, like the existence of a mad uncle in Cleethorpes. As a novice you must *hint* at having done a bit and do some fictional name dropping, Knox-Johnston, Clare Francis, Portland Bill etc. For a male novice the monthly Men's Night is the time of test, this being an occasion when men line the bar three deep and lie through their teeth about past exploits.

You should arm yourself with an I-remember-the-time story. All around you members will be seeking a lull in the hubbub. 'That reminds me . . . I remember the time when . . . I'll never forget the night when . . .' they chorus eagerly. Make sure that your story cannot be challenged. Never name *places.* A reference to Scapa Flow for instance is liable to be seized upon by a turkey-necked Founder-Member with a reedy voice and a rattling denture who starts going on about tides.

Failing a story of your own, hitch a ride on somebody else's. Wait for the climax and then give a short, barking laugh and say 'How true. My God, how true . . . !'

Nobody either boasts about or asks about another's qualifications or tastes. To do so can prove to be highly embarrassing, like inviting a daughter's shy boyfriend to share the Sunday chicken then asking whether he's a leg or a breast man.

What kind of club?

The local sailing club

This can be a tin-roof and tea-urn affair whose members are mainly in the late stages of puberty and therefore all lung, leg and lager. They race dinghies with croaking disregard for any law except getting back first and getting away with it at the gybing mark.

It will be up a creek somewhere, approached by a dirt road with ruts like World War I trenches. At intervals, working parties fill these with rocks which impart a mighty rolling motion to vehicles and mother's neck has never been the same since.

Boisterous good humour and clouds of steam typify weekends. Races are started and finished with derisive raspberries from aerosol fog horns. The voluntary club cleaner has never, in all her life, seen anything as disgusting as the men's ablutions. Yet another notice on the board confirms this.

There is an 'active cruiser class' – a designation hinting at Geiger-counters. There is one owner who wins everything in every race every year which wins him the undying hatred of the losers who 'don't take it so *seriously* for God's sake!' What that man spends on sails they dread to think.

There will be an annual Dinner Dance above a pub where 'that boy' should never have been allowed beer *and* wine. She'll never get the stains out of that back seat and while we're at it where did they buy that fearful claret?

Town yacht club

Everybody is made welcome by a *paid* club secretary. He gives in his notice about every three months having had it up to here with being treated like *dirt* by you-know-who. He would let in a party of Dyak head-hunters provided they wore ties, signed the book and upped the bar takings.

The club was founded in 1925 and designed by an architect whose mother had been frightened by a blancmange. Visiting yachties can have showers without feeling that they are suspected of nicking teaspoons and ladies are welcome – *to what* is not clear.

There is a cruiser section, a cadet section and bridge on Wednesdays.

Windsurfers must keep clear of the line and no wet-suits are allowed in the bar unless ties are worn.

There are very few social rules. Men ease their bottoms an inch above their chairs when a lady joins the table and you don't order a toasted cheese sandwich when the barman is going flat out with both hands like a robot spot-welder.

The cadet section is presided over by a harassed volunteer who is all too conscious of the exploding puberty around him. It is no easy matter to teach twelve stone of wobbling female adolescence how to roll-tack without actually touching . . . 'Try to get your bod . . . er . . . self a bit further inboard by sliding your bot . . . er . . . seat etc etc'.

The ROYAL clubs

These are GOOD clubs and you don't just *join* them. The usual rigmarole of being proposed and seconded (Oh thanks old man, make it a double) doesn't just get you in, like enrolling for badminton in the village hall. There is a club Selection Committee whose job it is to review your application and keep you out. 'We must consider this next application With Care!' says the Chairman, thereby putting the boot in. It is a process smacking of sheepdogs and men in gum-boots swiping with their caps.

A GOOD club allows its members to 'wear a defaced ensign' which sounds like some freaky nightie upon which a moustache has been pencilled. It may vary from the sort of club in which men wear mess-jackets, sport massive bushy eyebrows and have just got back from somewhere remote, to the scuffed leather furniture and senile steward kind. 'We ought to let him go!' members whisper, implying an open cage door and a quick flutter of dusty wings.

Although GOOD clubs proclaim themselves open to all (sic) and members are jolly good sorts, the casual cruising visitor clutching towel, clean change and shower-gel may find a welcome like a victim of the black plague in Out-patients. Ten marble steps, a half-acre of polished parquet and pillars brings them face to face with a club servant whose lips are turned permanently inboard with distaste.

Father, with foresight, may be wearing his club tie, much as some intrepid exorcist might hold aloft a crucifix as he enters the ruined crypt. Or perhaps as an explorer might proffer his paltry trade goods to some fierce and proud tribal chief. It is the tie of the Pinner Cruising and Social Club.

'Perhaps sir will sign the visitor's book *and include sir's full address*,' says the club servant in Imperial tones.

The VERY GOOD Royal Yacht Clubs exist in dwindling numbers due to a hyperactive Great Reaper. Membership and obituary columns run in tandem. Nodding old gentlemen lost in cavernous chairs wait grimly to take over each other's lockers. On the smoke-yellowed walls past Commodores in wing collars and vast yachting caps gaze down on dusty trophies. A dusty steward with a shaky hand sprinkles recumbent members with brandy-and-soda as if administering some form of blessing.

New club members

Let us assume that our little family (which sounds like pygmies, bones through noses etc) have been accepted as members of a well-established local yacht club and the Trout parents are about to make their first appearance. The young Trouts will be attending Cadet Evening later on, where they will be struck numb, rendered zombie-like and bereft of speech by sucking at Coke tins. Later they will join in general debate about which TV programmes are the most *boring*.

On this first occasion for Gerald and Miriam *appearances* are critical. Open neck shirts and vivid anoraks are closely akin to looking for lodgings with a drum-kit under your arm, but they mustn't over-do it either. Boat-cloaks are out and so are white flannels. The ideal might be quality blazers (without badges on pockets), designer slacks and a pair of raddled, blasted and faded canvas shoes are recommended.

They should choose a busy evening. On a quiet evening their shy and hesitant entry – like the mottled roe-deer timorously entering some forest glade – will either subject them to a long scrutiny by members at the bar – 'Oh Lor, new members!' – or they will be left alone to wander around looking at trophies in cases, portraits of founders and the instructions on fire extinguishers.

On a busy evening the club or social secretary will note their arrival as if heralded by a roll of drums. 'Lovely!' he enthuses falsely, 'Always nice to see new faces, marvellous. Let me buy you a drink.' Both order modestly. They are then guided upon a round of high-speed introductions, nodding and smirking like clockwork cobblers, while a string of names passes into limbo via one ear and out of the other.

The members who have been party to this little exercise in social benevolence swing back to the bar, duty done, names forgotten. '. . . As I was saying . . .' they resume, booming into their pints. The secretary dashes off to deal with the steward who has just tendered his notice again and the Trouts are left to study a notice about items left in the changing room. Their owners must collect them by next Saturday. Then the club bore pounces.

It is a lady of commanding appearance with an Easter Island Statue profile whose jutting chin is adorned by a solitary hair like a palm tree on some tropical atoll. She speaks in a series of barks.

'What have you got, hah!' she demands to know. Miriam, taken aback, begins murmuring something about her sinuses. Gerald confesses that they are thinking about a little cruiser.

'You need a Dabchick, man, buy a Dabchick!' she barks. She needs to have a word with the secretary. The Trouts are left to study the portraits. All are wearing gigantic yachting caps and sitting rigidly bolt upright as if fearful for the stability of these tottering confections. The Race Officer takes over. 'Little cruiser eh,' he says, 'We've got a keen Unrated Cruiser Class.' It sounds vaguely disreputable, like being unchurched or ineligible to join the Freemasons. 'They race for fun,' he explains, 'Nothing *serious*.'

In truth when the Unrated Cruiser Class races, owners could not be more serious if they were helmeted, blacked-up and firing from the hip.

Joining in

The new member who uses the club as somewhere to leave the dinghy oars, drifting in and out wraith-like or exchanging the odd nod when meeting another member in the convenience creates a strained atmosphere. On the other hand the new member who hurls him/herself into every activity, joins every committee, every working party and roster, attends all the rallies, acts as Father Christmas and takes over the tea urn soon becomes either relied upon utterly or regarded as an infernal busybody who hasn't been here ten minutes. (And who the hell does he/she think he/she is anyway?) It must be done slowly but resolutely like closing the front door on a Jehovah's Witness. The Trouts might do worse than sign up for the club Cruise-in-Company. Although perhaps not a lot.

The Cruise-in-Company

The general aim of this exercise is to get the novice cruiser owners to sea with the moral support of the more experienced members but since novices tend to remain incognito, their unmasking sees them instantly surrounded by eager attendants like a prisoner being hurried out of court under a blanket.

Gerald Trout, adopting a posture of relaxed and casual expertise, keeps quiet. He leaves the first buoy on the wrong hand, runs shudderingly up the putty and has to be pulled off by a laconic boatman. 'You'll soon pick it up, sir,' this expert howls comfortingly above the engine din and for all to hear. Unwittingly he reduces his tip by half.

The fleet will consist of a mixture of vessels. The owners of large, fast ones make a great and ostentatious show of 'slowing down' for the *slow* boats, letting sails flap and lowering headsails, all of which infuriates those who are nursing every quarter-knot out of their rotund and lolloping vessels. 'Ah,' their owners say, wagging heads, 'but our boat is a *sea-boat,* she has a comfortable motion.' The slower you go the more comfortable it gets, until you become a lighthouse. 'Just wait until it blows a bit, that's all!' they smirk sourly, 'Oh yes, just you wait . . . !'

From the moment the fleet is under way every owner switches on his VHF radio, picks up his hand-set and, adopting a sort of nasal drawl, commences a non-stop dialogue of utter twaddle. Strict procedure degenerates rapidly. The world becomes richer for knowing that there will be scotch eggs for lunch aboard *Little Auk* and 'I say again all after 'little'.

The destination may be foreign or a more modest foray just up the coast. Going foreign means The Meal Ashore. It is an hour and innumerable aperitifs and bread rolls late in arriving by which time all are speaking fluent French, even those who don't know any. They just happen to be in Holland. It takes as long again to sort out *l'addition* and who-had-what. Chairs are on

tables and the waiter has his hat on. He accepts the tip
with a hiss of gratitude.

A sail up the coast usually ends with the boats all
rafted up alongside each other, which offers about as
much privacy as a bus station but allows owners to visit
one another. It is a scene of dizzy activity not unlike
those sultry evenings when flying ants make a
simultaneous decision to swarm. ('Hey, let's swarm,
fellers!')

Bodies scuttle in and out of forehatches, bent upon
admiring each other's tip-up washbasins. Cousin Mabel,
who has been a bit run-down lately, is caught in the
toilet. It had seemed a good time to go. There she sits,
gripping the door handle on the inside while inquisitive
visitors wrestle with it on the outside. She will not yield.
It is like a re-enactment of the Defence of Rorkes Drift.
'Stand firm, lads, here the devils come again!'

The nadir, as social occasions go, is drinks aboard the Commodore's yacht where the barriers are down. All contribute to the fun. Gerald Trout rises to his feet. 'Oh God, NOT the animal impressions,' prays Miriam. He invites the company to join him down on the farm. 'Here comes old Rover the sheepdog . . .' he announces, clearing his throat . . . The evening will end with a sing-song, inadequately fuelled on minimal quantities of flat beer and a dozen salted peanuts per head. *Ten Green Bottles* is followed by *Old MacDonald Had a Farm*. 'Eeee-iii-eee-ii-oooooooooo' mourn the revellers as if at some ancient Celtic wake.

Joining the committee

No new member should seek election to the club committee *actively*. This might be interpreted as being pushy. An expression of interest in its dreary machinations is all that is required to get on it (which makes it sound like some sort of bicycle).

Essentially a club committee is a small group of people who meet at intervals to exchange anecdotes, these being triggered off by the various items on the agenda. Thus item four 'alterations to ladies shower' gives rise to a dissertation on Alderney Race in a weather-going force six and item five 'advert for new steward' gives us the latest on my wife's knee and the waiting time for new hips.

If every raconteur had his/her way they'd be coming home with the milkman. It takes a good Chairman (something on telly at ten) to conduct a tight meeting. A good Chairman (oh alright, or woman) can rattle through the minutes as if auctioning fat hoggits and have you out in the street halfway through your first doodle and wondering what the hell to do with the rest of the evening. While matters arising are usually of such staggering banality that no real debate is expected, *serious* issues are dealt with in the local boozer, *ex officio* and in the absence of opposition to be confirmed in committee later by a show of hands.

Occasionally committee members are detailed to form a steering committee with the task of steering an earlier steering committee, like some form of blindfolded conga. They leave the meeting and forget all about it until the day before the next meeting. Hasty phone calls are made. Far more serious is when there is a call for a volunteer.

A club representative is needed to attend some area seminar of stultifying boredom. 'Perhaps we can have a volunteer?' says the Chairman resignedly. He might as well be asking for a bungee-jumper. Members stiffen in their seats. Rows of identical expressions confront him like TV sets in a shop window. Just as the fledglings of some ground-nesting fowl will freeze at the approach of a predator, relying upon protective colouration, endeavouring to merge with the background foliage, they slide down smoothly in their chairs. They merge with some difficulty. Muriel, anaemic from childhood, cops for a fire extinguisher.

'Surely *somebody* can manage it?' wheedles the Chairman. Nobody can. They pretend to consult their diaries. Any other day would have been fine, they sigh collectively.

The new member's aim should be to avoid doing a specific job and most of all to avoid being Treasurer, resisting flattery and the blandishments of those who don't want the job. The title, redolent of glittering piles of wealth in iron-bound chests, has little glory attached to it. The club Treasurer works at home, occupying half the table ten minutes before 'she' wants to lay the cloth for supper. The day before the meeting he/she 'does' the figures. A term open to interpretation, which is why so many of them resign in high dudgeon (sounds like a Cotswold village) having been called to task at the AGM by some nit-picking, calculator-pecking out-of-town member with a ginger moustache.

The true peaks of oratory, however, are reserved for AOB at AGMs. You get two members in violent opposition, both with plum-rich complexions and quivering chins howling each other down via The Chair. All remarks made in committee must be routed through The Chair. It comes to a pretty pass when folk start yelling at the furniture.

Working parties

Gerald Trout may well be invited to join a working party. As a gesture of good-fellowship it is an invitation which he should accept with a show of pleasure. 'Cementing the ladies toilets! I'd love to,' he enthuses, filled with eager anticipation. Working parties are co-opted with relentless determination. Filling in potholes, spreading gravel, mending the dinghy racks and painting the club launch are stern male matters; the ladies scrub, wipe down and polish under equal duress. Let us examine a typical working schedule:

Painting the club launch
0915   Assemble at the job.
1000   Begin work.
1030   Ten minute coffee break.
1100   Begin work again.
1200   Club bar open.
1430   Back from bar (lunch).
1500   Dew begins falling. Stop work.

Working parties requiring tools are subject to delay while sandpaper is being torn into scraps the size of sticking plasters. You get four men waiting to use one scraper.

Social occasions

There is the Grand Annual Dinner and Dance, a Moss Bros benefit and a meal of unparalleled mediocrity which is 'one of the chances she gets to go out and *make something of herself*' (and need-we-stay-for-the-dancing?). There are also the Laying Up and the Fitting Out Suppers. While the latter are scarcely to be described as glittering social occasions, calling for blusher and eye-shadow, they are well supported.

Men's Supper Night is another convivial occasion where support plays a vital role. It is a bibulous ordeal involving sausage and mash and enough best bitter to float a pontoon. As the last chorus of *Nellie Dean,* sung with huge fervour in the gents' latrine where there is a fine echo, dies away to a groan, Gerald gets his coat and escapes. It is over his head and he is trying to shove one hand through a pocket. An arm is suddenly flung around his shoulders and a red-faced wagging head is thrust to within two inches of his own.

'Sherishly o' man, sherishly . . . you can trush me. Can't you trush me eh?'

Gerald winces as the breath hits him. 'Yesh I can trush, truss you,' he assures his fellow member. A snore is the only reply. Locked together like Greek dancers the pair make it to the street.

'No way. NO WAY!' says the taxi-driver, eyeing the dishevelled, swaying figures. Their shirts are out and their ties are cropped short. 'No way at all!' he vows, shuddering and accelerating simultaneously.

The walk home will be remembered dimly for an intolerable profusion of lamp-posts followed by repeated stabs at a door with a latchkey. With shoes-in-hand, standing on the dog (who shouldn't have been there in the first place) and on tip-toe, Gerald has made it.

'Why are you trying to get into the broom cupboard, Gerald?' comes a hard and hacksaw voice. Blessed oblivion follows on winged feet.

The winter programme

If any member banks on being able to stay home on wet nights then he/she has another think coming. A Social Secretary will have organised a series of *divertissements*. Failure to turn up without a good excuse for absence earns the charge of 'not being a very good club member'. Supporting the Programme is a duty, like giving blood and selling flags on Lifeboat Day.

A course of navigation classes is laid on by the Commodore described with Machiavellian cunning as 'Brush up your Nav Skills'; this makes them acceptable to *all*, even those of such howling but secret incompetence that they couldn't navigate out of a supermarket checkout and won't discuss Mercator's Projection in front of the children.

Not to be outdone, the Commodore's Lady organises a ladies aerobics class where a dozen fair members in leotards – bumblebees on the heroic scale – bound thunderously to music. Plaster rains down on the bar below like the snow scene in *Uncle Tom's Cabin*. A consultant builder is called in to pronounce on the structural health of the clubhouse. He wears a yellow Wimpy hat and rolls his own, sad little squibs like the pupae of the sort of moth that clogs things up. He's not 'appy about yer joists, squire, not 'appy at all and isn't afraid to say so. Five thousand quid should see you all right.

Yoga is suggested instead. 'That would put me in a difficult position!' says the Commodore's Lady prophetically.

Chapter Five

Anchoring

Let's anchor tonight
Oh what a delight
That is, apart from the nagging.
It takes one little rumble
Then wives start to grumble,
'Get up please and see if we're dragging!'

Homo Sapiens may have put a telescope into space, harnessed the atom and perfected keyhole surgery but we also invented the anchor – which is just about as scientific as charming away warts. It shows as dismal a lack of ingenuity as soap-on-a-rope or the plastic eggcup. Down the ages countless ships, proceeding rapidly backwards to destruction, should have tipped us the wink that we were on to a duff idea. Lowering a hook in the forlorn hope that it may somehow stick into the seabed is like trying to spear the last pickled onion in the jar with a knitting needle.

The very fact that we are continually reinventing the anchor should be proof that we're on a hiding to nowhere. All we get are successive generations of cursing sailors hopping, howling and sucking flattened thumbs. Anchors should carry government health warnings; if they don't rupture you, slip your discs or strain your heart, then you'd best start counting your fingers.

Anchor handling

You delegate.

Equipment

Every off-the-shelf cruiser comes ready-equipped with a 'bower' anchor which is small enough to be handled easily plus thirty metres of rope. This allows it to reach the seabed in thirty metres of water. An optional extra is a 'kedge' anchor which is just a pocket-sized bower. It can be carried out in the dinghy and dumped in a 100 metres of water for all the good it's going to do you. Large yachts may be equipped with a windlass for hauling in the anchor, smaller yachts are equipped with friends and relatives in yellow Marigold gloves who work at about the same speed that grass grows. The curious carvings to be found on many tillers are in fact teeth marks.

The tyro may hear frequent references to 'scope', eg 'Does she need more of it, shall I give her a bit more . . .

how much does she like? etc etc'. This is a personal and private matter. Just walk away.

Anchorages

There are a number of classifications as follows:

Popular or **Confrontational** Invites pre-breakfast encounters with irascible old men in sagging pyjamas.

Peaceful Haunts of coot and tern. Also Col (Ret) Narp self-appointed guardian of the lesser pied shag's nesting site.

God-it's-stopped! Follows sudden engine silence. Typically athwart the harbour ferry route and blocking the fishermen's fuelling jetty.

Just-for-lunch Just-for-about-48-hours of 30° rolling while awaiting arrival of diver. A favourite dumping ground for wire hawsers in WW2.

Suicidal Why, this bay is a perfect little sun-trap! Shingle seabed, rocks on three sides, wind shift imminent.

Prohibited Naval gunnery range. 'Why look, Gerald, there are whales spouting all around us!'

Anchoring techniques: bringing up[1]

If an anchorage appears to be crowded, remember, there is always room for just one more. It is a good plan to make an initial circuit of the area to assess its potential. Other yachts may appear to be deserted, but this is not so; some people are shy. Sound your foghorn and hail each by name. For example:

'Ahoy *Chocolate Chip,* what sort of bottom have you?'
'Ahoy *Sea Slug,* how's your water?'
'Ahoy *Little Pipit,* have you given her plenty?'

Having chosen your gap go for it boldly and let go with plenty of way on: this will ensure that the anchor digs well in. Let 'the more the merrier' be your slogan. Remember a cheery wave to your new neighbours at bow and stern. Bring your new portable radio up on deck so that all (especially the neighbours) can join in listening to 'Mo and the Morons'.

In a secluded anchorage it is customary for the first arrivals to hide behind their galley and loo curtains to watch the approach of other boats. This is a small but pleasant ritual. 'That's right!' they will snarl, 'Oh *very* nice. That's right, come and anchor *right* on top of us!' Each new arrival goes through this quaint ceremony.

An arriving yacht, her crew seeking social intercourse, may in fact anchor close by a solitary earlier arrival with the intention of 'making their number' as the saying goes.

'Ning,' the new arrival may say, 'Thought I'd just make my number.'

'Thought you'd make what?'

'My number. Thought I'd make it.'

'Make it what?'

The dialogue can be discontinued at this point.

When approaching an anchorage at night, a host of twinkling lights may greet the newcomer. These are the 'riding lights' of the assembled yachts already at anchor – a charming old gesture of welcome based upon the

---

[1] The reader is free to exercise his/her vile sense of humour.

belief that such lights would act as a guide for wandering fairies or, as the old couplet has it: 'Fairy, fairy, don't fly past, come rest your wings upon my mast'. It is considered a friendly response to call out 'Ahoy there, any fairies aboard?' as you motor past.

Should there be any doubt as to where the deepest water is to be found, you can hardly go wrong by choosing to anchor in the middle of the channel between the buoys. The coasters, trawlers and tripper boats will also choose the middle which is a good guide to the deepest water. Do not be misled by the fact that other yachts seem to cluster along the edges of the channel, this is only because they don't have enough rope to anchor in deeper water. You with your 30 metres (almost 100 feet!) will have no such worries.

The first anchorage

Now let us see how the Trouts tackle their first anchorage. They have given the Pilot book careful study. 'How about this then?' asks Miriam. 'This anchorage has EC Wed, Gs, DSl, Slp, Ch, el and sh?' 'Or,' counters Gerald, 'There's Poltroons Pool. Peaceful ancg amidst saltings, rich wildlife, gd hldg in min 2m with shlt S-NW. No shps or fclts?' It also suggests a venue far from critical eyes. Miriam suggests that if the gas runs out then don't blame her and don't grizzle about powdered milk and crackers in lieu of brown wholemeal. He comes on heavy with the Master Under God bit and so Poltroons Pool it shall be and crackers or lump-it.

Arriving at the approaches they follow Bns p and s, keeping prom yell hse in line Doom Point 278° True, ploughing to a halt in sft oz. There is another yell hse, only this one is a bit yellower. Borne onward again by the chuckling young flood (it knew something that they didn't), they reach the anchorage, a scene of limpid tranquillity flanked by bosky woods which echo to the laughter of the lesser spotted woodpecker (who also knew something etc, etc). About forty other yachts are sharing the limpid tranquillity. 'Why look!' cries Bosco, 'There's a yacht anchored further up.' And so there is. It is Col (Ret) Narp, champion of lesser shags, inventor of a huge cork to be hammered into the Channel Tunnel on French National Holidays and who was once mentioned in dispatches, at length and libellously.

With drumming engine and a fine fat flood tide under them they make a brave sight. 'Stand by your anchor!' commands Gerald sternly. Bosco goes forward and stands by it. Nothing else, just stands by it. The skipper is assessing speed over ground, distances and time with the skill born of sitting for long hours on a Polytechnic plastic chair. 'Let go anchor!' comes the stirring cry. There is some delay.

The Colonel, camera in hand, was in the act of zooming in on a lesser shag as it performed some sort of idiotic courtship dance when Bosco's left earhole, in close-up, loomed into shot. 'The nest by George!' the Colonel exclaimed, shutter clicking. 'A little miracle of moss, twigs and fluff. Why, the RSPB shall hear of this!'

Moorings, trots and piles[2]

Although listed anchorages are now largely given over to a profusion of permanent moorings, should any of the buoys be unoccupied the stranger is free to use them. The unexpected return of the rightful owner or tenant may lead to a laughing exchange of views and win you new friends. Or it may not . . .

Visitors' Buoys Many areas are provided with Visitors' Buoys. These are a form of bait laid by the Harbour Master in much the same way as a jam jar of sugary water is set out for the snaring of wasps. Twice a day the HM, cash till ringing merrily, makes a round of his traps. Visitors' Buoys are often spherical and painted white by both the harbour authority and the herring gulls and clearly marked ISIT, VIST or SIT S. They also

[2] Yes, yes alright!

resemble the warping buoys laid to facilitate visiting coasters in getting clear of quay or jetty.

Here a warning. This manoeuvre is most likely to occur at 2 am and a yacht moored to such a buoy in error is liable to receive a visit from a coaster mate with a vicious hangover, sculling a boat and towing a rusty wire rope. The yachtsman in his Paisley patterned jim-jams may then be addressed as follows:

'Wot the hiccough are you hiccoughers doin' on this hiccoughin' buoy?'

A reasoned attempt at explaining may fail.

'. . . an' don't give me none of yer hiccoughin' lip mush. Right!'

Pick-ups and private buoys Mooring buoys are either large and must be moored *to* or they are pick-ups which have to be lifted aboard and hauled tight. In many crowded anchorages these may be found laid for the convenience of visitors. They may have an anchor symbol on them to indicate that they are a substitute for anchoring. Make sure that the rope is pulled up really tight. This will keep your stern just clear of the bows of the next boat in line astern and ensure a really good night's rest.

If in the absence of a Visitors' Buoy or a pick-up you are obliged to occupy a private buoy (with the name of the boat on it) be prepared to vacate it. Simply drop your anchor and let go of the buoy. Some experienced sailors have occult powers which enable them to sense when the owner of the mooring is navigating the Straits of Magellan or stuck on a rock off Sark and subject to a delay in returning.

The novice is less gifted. He/she also walks down man-holes and gets the bun with the finger bandage in it. The rightful buoy owner is at that very moment thumping up-river wet, cold, hungry and in a vile mood.

'Nighty night all,' cries our tyro, zipping up his bag, 'Me for a spot of zizz!' It will be him for a spot of slapping around barefoot on deck, and an emergency departure, pyjamas around ankles, tiller in one hand and teeth in the other.

A useful tip: When turning in on a mooring whose owner may/may not return unexpectedly, simply place your cap on the saloon table and stow your dentures in it. This will ensure that they are ready to ship, that your diction and enunciation are clear and that your orders are intelligible. 'Fuff astern and leff go foffard,' is liable to misinterpretation.

Another useful tip: Make certain that it is *your* cap and not somebody else's as there have been some distreffing cayfeffs of scalp woundffs.

Useful note: The rings on the tops of buoys are specially designed so that they will turn themselves sideways-on as you approach. This feature is to frustrate the users of clever-dick patent clip-on boathooks.

On the trot

With this mooring arrangement yachts lie like a string of beads with mooring buoys or piles interposed, thus an arrival must endeavour to attach ropes both fore and aft, simultaneously and in a fresh beam wind. There may be more amusing shows but not many. Faust-on-ice is one of them.

There was one memorable case in which mother had the tips of her toes hooked over the bow pulpit, and her

boathook at full reach while father was hauling in aft and crying out for another inch. The wife's brother (down for the day, and never again thank you very much) featured yet another Golden Gem when his arms and legs got wrapped round the piles while the boat was circling for a fourth attempt.

Yachts may also 'raft up' alongside each other on the trots. The crews of yachts which end up in the middle had better take out local library tickets.

Privacy is at a premium. People pull their little curtains and forgo cockpit ablutions or worse. They congregate below to discuss their neighbours. There is an odd-looking couple in the green boat and do you think they are . . . you know? Or, on the other hand, hospitality may be the order of the day. There will be drinks and Marmite fingers. The aim is to keep them on the wine box or *they'll never go* (a nice hospitable little touch we must say!). With a wine box a host can make a great production out of eviscerating the silver plastic bag and wringing the last drop out of it, perhaps even resorting to surgery with galley scissors. A guest who can't take that sort of hint merits one firm hand on the collar and another on the seat of the pants.

A yacht may also be moored between her own anchors in a manoeuvre colourfully called 'the running moor', which offers more scope for baring the soul and

revealing personal shortcomings than a cardboard confessional. It is not recommended for beginners.

Having selected his/her berth the exponent comes
clipping in with crew stationed both fore and aft. On
the stern is a huge heap of rope to which is attached the
kedge. On a command of LET GO AFT the kedge is
hurled overboard, the rope zipping after it, snaking and
whistling astern while its attendant leaps and prances in
a spirited tarantella of self-preservation. It must not be
allowed to snag. It snags.

'IT'S SNAGGED!' shrills the skipper, poking at it.
The rope is humming like a barbershop quartet. Then
away it goes taking with it a locker lid and a welly. There
remains but to 'middle-on-both'. *Muddle* on both
would be a fairer description. You end up hard aground
with a line round the fan and a cockpit full of rope, mud
and wriggly jelly things.

This dissertation upon mooring would not be complete without a reference to The Sunflower Moor. Also
known as a Recipe for Divorce. It is a favourite with
club rallies. Take thirty yachts and anchor them in a circle, alongside each other and bows facing outwards.
Take thirty skippers of icy calm, bushy eyebrows and
clipped enunciation. Take also thirty wives, ten of whom
have said that this is the very last time she sails with him
and *did you hear me!* Add a 180° wind shift and light
blue touch paper.

Chapter Six

Berthing

Going alongside
May be the wrong-side.
Then life becomes a bit fraught,
And the toerail to starboard
Folds up like cardboard,
When you've hung all your fenders to port.

The approach to a berth alongside, a town quay or commercial dock may be preceded by an exchange of signals at the harbour entrance where a man in a white shirt opens a window, shouts and waves his fist. This indicates that you have just broken a byelaw.

On such occasions, where vocal explanation is impractical and VHF communication leads to a muffled and angry exchange of working channels, a sort of radio hunt-the-slipper, it is best to fall back on the Oh-silly-little-me routine. Try to radiate an atmosphere of simple family innocence. The Trouts have The Boy as their ace in the hand. In full scout uniform, leader of the Whimbrel Patrol, he stands in the bow pulpit giving his patrol cry of 'Whimmmmmmbrel' accompanied by the classic mating behaviour of flapping wings and jerking head. Harbour officials will be deeply affected by this dramatic exhibition.

A berth should be chosen within reach of such essential supplies as an off-licence and hairdresser ('My hair feels *disgusting!*'), which means the Town Quay where you will have to stare up the nostrils of spectators at low tide, and cower behind your curtains at high.

The Trouts will have had no problem. What a spot of luck eh! Bang under the storm drain. There comes a flatulent rumble of thunder and the imminent prospect of a cockpit full of mud, Coke tins, a dead rat and quantities of those curiously pink and bloated earthworms peculiar to floodwater.

The expert runs out mooring lines at speed and with economy, not so your tyro – book-in-hand, working away with a mission, he rapidly weaves a delicate web of rope round his boat.

It is like some humble insect spinning its cocoon, later to emerge in a brilliant metamorphosis of gossamer wing and questing antennae. Head and stern lines, breast ropes, crossed springs and a hauling-off kedge in case of onshore hurricanes are laid and minutely adjusted. 'She won't get away from that!' he forecasts unwisely. Up comes the Harbour Master on his bike, all cap, scowl and trouser-clip. 'You can't lie 'ere, sir!' he cries joyfully.

In the wet basin

Not surprisingly this is a dock or basin and wet. It is kept so by means of lock gates which are open briefly twice a day around high tide with the predictable result that twice a day they are as busy as Santa's Wonderful Workshop. Immediately prior to opening, with one gate still shut, a collection of yachts can be found circling aimlessly, like people outside a long-occupied phone kiosk, rattling their loose change, whistling and kicking stones. Do not let this apparent lassitude fool you. They are taut as bowstrings.

The goal is to have your boat aimed at the opening and in front of everybody else when the gate opens. Gerald Trout, dry-lipped, his tongue feeling as if it were hand-knitted in rug wool, juggles his throttle. Why can't he get closer? is what Miriam wants to know. He explains, croakingly, that she has no idea . . . that she doesn't understand and don't bloody distract him!

'Oh charming!' she blasts back in *that* voice. 'Because I'm only a woman, hey? Hah? Oh very nice!'

The gates swing open. They are facing the wrong way. They go belting in after everybody else with a storm cloud hovering above the crosstrees. It is like the Autumn Sales rush, amazing bargains at unbelievable prices and trousers that split up the crutch first time on. A dozen engines bellow their message of naked power, exhaust echoes hammer back from the confining walls as yachts race to get a berth near the cafés and away from the fishmarket. 'Ici, ici!' commands an official in a beret directing them towards the fish market.

They'll need to raft up alongside one another. Crews dangle fenders as if bobbing for apples. It is commonly accepted that smaller yachts should lie outside larger ones. Two yachts of equal size race to get there first.

'I think you'll be more comfortable outside us!' cry both skippers harmonising in a duet. Stern gears scream. The Harbour Master remembers an urgent appointment. In the approach to a berth a wise skipper will explain to his crew which side he intends to lay alongside, but the tyro has about as much hope of making so precise a forecast as he has of predicting Armageddon. The following little hint is based upon many years of barefaced falsehood.

With a crew loaded with fenders and ropes and bouncing around on their toes like goalkeepers facing a penalty kick, the skipper must resort to subterfuge. Holding handkerchief to lips in a simulated cough he says, *indistinctly*. 'Star*port* side to!'

Later, when the echoes have died away, when the guardrail has been reshipped and the toerail booted back into place he can dissemble. It seems that he never said 'starboard side to'. What he said was '*thar* port side to'. There are other ways of becoming a contemptible, mean, lying little squirt but not many easier ones.

With your wet basin the time to watch is when a gate begins to *close*. It is like bolting the cat-flap. Luckless pussy comes barreling down the garden path and the next thing you know it is wearing its tail like a muff.

The strange marina

Since the reader probably berths his boat in a marina and is accustomed to curling toes and popping eyes we will skate over the basic techniques of manoeuvring in and out. Distances will have been judged, turning circles estimated and stopping room plotted. It is a matter of acquiring a new skill, and comparable to eating spaghetti in the dark with chopsticks.

While away, cruising new and strange marinas pose a challenge to one's skills. At the height of the season finding a marina berth is not always easy. 'Why is it that other people can always find a berth and we can't?' lady-wife wants to know, having had all she can take of coots and terns, slopping around in mud and LOOK at the state of her box-pleats!

It is best done while at sea and by VHF radio. There will be audible teeth-sucking and weary sighs but they will see what they can do, which means a Visitor's Berth at the far end of a heaving, clanking, grinding pontoon where you will heave, grind and clank.

There is a strict embargo on the use of yacht toilets in harbour and a ten minute walk to the ablutions. Father, an early-morning man and regular as clock-work, can be seen hurtling along the pontoon with pumping knees and slapping flip-flops at a rate that might jeopardise all 100 metre spring records.

'I just hope he makes it that's all!' says mother with fervour, up on the coachroof and shading her eyes. She hasn't the facilities and she doubts if even her Super-Plus Automatic Whizzo with added Bio-Whitener could cope.

All marinas are designed on the same principle – the 'pitcher plant' concept. This is an elongated tube which lures luckless insects to a sticky doom at the bottom end.

The visitor yachtsman in search of a berth and failing to find one must then endeavour to turn 180° in order

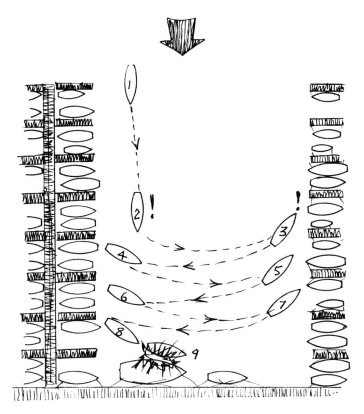

to escape from the lane. There are two methods for dealing with this situation, he can either put the helm hard-over, open the cocks and go for it, or attempt the zig-zags. Your pickle-eyed helmsman, mouth open in a silent scream, *may* bring off the helm-down turn. Spectators, lining the arena like vultures on the ghats, are confident that he won't.

Our diagram makes the zig-zags easily understandable. To and fro, to and fro, backwards and forwards in a movement reminiscent of a minuet from a statelier age, each 'set' taking the yacht further to leeward.

It is worth remembering that the saloon settee mattresses, the scatter cushions embroidered with little seahorses, and all the lifejackets stuffed into one sailbag make an effective and simple fender to cram into the rapidly narrowing gap betwixt topsides and dock. Damage may be minimal and mainly confined to father's cap, which he will be munching.

Storm-bound anchorage

When the yacht is careering round her anchor in a horizontal blast of rain and the mast is shrieking (being flogged with wet ropes is no hoot), when there is a dredger adrift upwind, when smacks are running for shelter, whole trees are being uprooted and the windows are streaming condensation like a Finnish sauna lacking only a damn good hiding with birch twigs, you'd never believe how cosy it can be down below.

Now is the time when you'll bless the moment you thought to put aboard a wide selection of card and board games, suitable for all ages and for four or more players. A warning must be given however. There may be a certain person in a position of authority, not a million miles away, who should know better. He may be a bell-ringer, carpet bowler and in line for a seat on the board but he is not above cheating something rotten. Watch the following games keenly.

Scrabble Unless you can dedicate one bunk for the accommodation of the Greater Oxford English Dictionary, this entertaining and instructive game may have to be shelved. It may well be that 'quuezzyquex' really is a mineral found in the Andes as *he* insists; on the other hand he may be lying through his teeth.

Monopoly (Also known as 'It's-only-a-game-for-God's-sake!') It should be agreed by all, right from the start, that while Old Kent Road and Whitechapel *may* offer rich development possibilities, in the context of the game their rents still aren't worth peanuts.

Chequers or chess You-know-who may find it necessary to rise suddenly and dash on deck to look at the anchor. This dedication to duty may coincide with a losing streak. G-clamps on the board are advised.

Snakes and ladders Watch intently!

There is no card game that is cheat-proof, which leaves only Happy Families and Tiddlywinks. There may be gaps in the floorboards and incestuous innuendos are not unknown.

Running maintenance

This is not, as the term might suggest, a quick gallop round the waterline with a brushful of boot-top paint but a periodic overhauling of working parts that don't. A day storm-bound at anchor offers an excellent opportunity for father to catch up on essential little jobs, and to get his own back on her for spring cleaning on the only day he's had off work this year for pity's sake! On that occasion the lady-wife with her head wrapped in a tea-towel and armed with a howling vacuum cleaner pursued him, morning paper in hand, from one chair to another. In vain, the lifted feet of co-operation. Sanctuary on the sofa was like Rockall in a force ten. With her duster on a stick, she hounded him to the final refuge – the wheelbarrow in his shed.

'Maintenance,' he pipes – at his most hateful and pompous with it – 'is for the good and the safety of all, and (a bitter laugh) don't imagine that I *enjoy* it!'

And so up comes the entire cabin sole so that he can 'look' at the seacocks (he sure as hell can't budge them).

Up comes the bunks and the engine box. It is like major road works ahead. All it lacks is a row of cones and winking lights, and maybe a tent with a kettle in it.

Imprisoned in the forecabin her only escape is via the forehatch. Rain drums away like Ringo Starr. In desperation she legs it over his inverted buttocks *en route* for the quarterberth.

'I'll need to get in there next,' he booms resonantly. It would seem that he has a nasty little drip from his stuffing gland – a malady suggesting a trip to the Health Centre and an uncomfortable examination with cold hands. It is also an opportunity to tidy out the chart table drawer. A magic colouring book, a shopping bag and a pair of doll's knickers having no apparent navigational value. He will also be able to hunt out the lost sausage from behind the gimballed cooker. It has been there since the night he offered to cook supper off Portland Bill, which nobody else either wanted to do or eat. It appears at extended intervals, like the Phantom of the Opera, in force five on port tack, furry as a prize angora and elusive as the Beast of Bodmin.

The dinghy tender

A dinghy large enough to contain the entire family or ship's company is an essential part of the cruising scene. With a suitable outboard motor it serves as a ferry from an anchorage to the shore or, given a break in the weather, a tour of the anchorage can be enjoyed by all. Father will entertain and educate his little band by commenting on other craft, pointing out the absurdity of this rig or that and drawing attention to the hideous colour schemes to be seen. They can share a good laugh at the idiotic names given by some owners to their boats, secure in the knowledge that the roar of the outboard prevents others from being a party to his remarks.

Earlier generations used wooden tenders which had to be towed everywhere, butting the parent vessel up the fantail and banging against the topsides all night. Crews would feign sleep, knowing that father, sorrowing for his paintwork, would crack in the end and pad around on deck cursing and fixing it. A favourite and well-loved jest was to cry out 'Morning, I see you've got a tender behind!' The jokester would then fall about, sobbing with mirth. 'Oh my deary Lor!' he might cry, gasping for breath at his own rich drollery.

The advent of the inflatable dinghy, a sort of monstrous whoopee cushion, with its pump, patches and little plastic paddles, has enabled many to go to sea who might otherwise have missed the opportunity. Especially when a stiff offshore breeze is blowing, with a duff outboard and a boat stuffed with people like olives on a pizza.

There are two types of inflatable dinghy: the semi-rigid with a large black engine which *zips* everywhere, usually driven by a child in a huge baseball cap, and the floppy, squashy sort like yours and mine. You'd stand a better chance of getting ashore dry-shod and box-pleats pristine with an outboard engine on an orthopaedic bed.

In the floppy sort your feet plunge around on the soft bottom like running in a nightmare, each forming little pools of water as you tread. Kneeling to start the outboard gets you two wet kneecaps. Passengers sit on the sidetubes facing inwards so that their bums are slapped by wavelets while being constantly dowsed by waves bursting over the bows; it is like a non-stop clown-and-whitewash act. Only the driver, crouching cravenly in the lee of his dripping spouse, remains dry.

The dinghy can be inflated on deck with a foot pump (designed for flat feet) which involves a sort of hippity-hop shuffle. Once fully inflated it will be realised that the floorboards should have been fitted prior to inflation so they have to be left out. The dinghy becomes a sort of maritime bouncy castle lacking only Co-Co the Laughable Clown and his side-splitting antics. It is not an omission likely to be missed if you forget to make fast the painter and the wind takes charge. The merry chase down harbour with stabbing boathook provides merriment in plenty.

After use it is usual to deflate the dinghy and restow it in the valise provided by a munificent manufacturer. It is too small. Dinghies only fit their valises in showrooms. Thereafter, and despite the entire crew crawling around on it trying to squeeze out the last bit of air, it fits like a fat lady trying on bargains at a Mammoth Sale, Prices Slashed.

An inflatable should NEVER be towed astern in a fresh following breeze. If it is triced up hard against the aft pulpit it is liable to whip up and over, clapping down over the cockpit like a biscuit tin lid – and who had all the Chocolate Bourbons is what I'd like to know?

Towed on a long painter, the consequences can be far-reaching. Witness the disturbing case in which a yacht was running for shelter up some marshy creek. The dinghy became airborne and wrapped itself around the backstay just above the helmsman's cringing neck. On the marshes Brigadier (Ret) Narp (whose brother we have met) showed no hesitation. 'By the living Jimmy it's the dreaded bald eagle!' he cried, giving it both barrels. The helmsman, cap riddled and smoking, danced and waved his twin-fisted gratitude. 'Feller's trying to thank me,' commented the Brigadier with typical modesty.

Outboard motors

Starting procedures vary. The big black sort give a snicker and roar into full, bellowing power. Yours and mine have to be humoured. They work perfectly in garden water butts and repair shop test tanks, prior to signing a fat cheque for yet another 'looking-at', or at any time when they are not really needed.

So you woo it with new plugs and air filters and you strain the fuel through gauze *and* three layers of Muriel's tights (which will whip the grin off her face when she sees them). You proceed to start it with applied skill. The first pull draws a beneficial gulp of explosive vapour into

its nasty little lungs chuffa-chuff. The next two pulls are more vigorous but equally non-productive. Then the third and chuffachuffffffff-ah.

'She fired, she fired!' everybody cries triumphantly.

Well that's it, isn't it? If it doesn't pick up after that then forget it, mate! It will remain as dead as a hedge-hog in the fast lane.

It is an all too familiar little tableau. Father jerking and cursing, mother sitting up forr'd with her shopping bag, head-scarf and eye-shadow while the small craft drifts tide-borne past anchored yachts with their appreciative audiences. She bestows royal waves left and right, smile painted on and lop-sided. Why doesn't he give up and *row* the bloody thing? she asks herself, why not use the *paddles*? 'Gooze the goody gaddles man?!' she grates, sideways, smiling falsely.

One last try, a BIG one. He rises to his sumo half-crouch, takes a firm hold and YANKS. It should have produced a fatter spark he reasons. All it produces is a howl from lady-wife who now has two loose front teeth. If he thinks he's going to enjoy his spare ribs and soy sauce tonight while she's supping away at bread-and-milk, then he's as dumb as a pot cuckoo.

Chapter Seven

Navigation

I compute my position
With great precision
To within half a cable.
But the sea makes me vomit
So I keep away from it,
And work on the kitchen table.

Considering the cost of getting to sea in your own boat, the break-neck efforts we make to get the hell off it again, while curious, hint at a need to take the shortest and quickest route possible.

Before the advent of peeping, squeaking, flickering electronic navigation aids, the art of the navigator in narrow waters was an imperfect science, an erratic crab-like progress. It had all the uncertainties of the novice ballroom dancer, progressing forwards, sideways and together, manoeuvring his charming partner as if steering a forklift truck and destined to fetch up in a corner among the potted palms.

It was always easy (still is) to detect the novice navigator at work. His/her head will be popping in and out of the hatch like a hen in a crate; he will be taking non-stop compass bearings. This is called 'fixing the position' and the chart will show an unbroken line of crosses like a badly cobbled-up rip. Between these bouts of activity, when sight of the land is lost, a 'dead reckoned' course is plotted.

Dead reckoning is dead inaccurate and dead boring, which means that people in days gone by forgot to keep it up and thereby often discovered new continents. It is worth bearing in mind that when Columbus discovered America he thought he was aiming for India – an unwelcome surprise not unlike a jogger inadvertently flushing a courting couple out of the long grass.

The steering compass

Ancient navigators, wishing to know in which direction the land lay, would dispatch a raven carried for this purpose. It was a ploy which filled the cabin with feathers, plastered the chart with foul excrement and resulted in a landfall up a tree. The method was discontinued in favour of half coconut shells and the like which were pretty useless unless you liked coconut cake.

The magnetic compass always points to magnetic north like a hound at a sausage counter and this is fine if you want to go to the magnetic north, which few people do. The steering compass is the navigator's best friend as it can be blamed for every discrepancy.

Since acting ability is an essential tool in the navigator's art (a good one can make Sir Richard Burton look like second shepherd in a school nativity play) the steering compass can be regarded as an accessory, like Hamlet's skull. The arrival of a landfall bang on schedule, which rates as rare as finding the six-toed sloth, is always an occasion for thespian display.

Conversely, the non-arrival of a landfall on schedule can be blamed on the compass and on the succession of bat-eared, fumbling, pathetic and witless helmsmen who have occupied the steering seat for the past twenty-four hours. It is the actor-navigator's finest hour. 'What's the use of *trying* to navigate?' he demands to know, features working convulsively. Little Nell is on her deathbed. A harsh sob breaks from him etc.

Chartwork

It is generally understood that the chart table is used on a timeshare basis by navigator, cook and kids. This means that the navigator must learn to practise his/her little miracles between a hot pan of spaghetti-in-tomato and the chicken drumsticks, with the parallel rules having a bumpy walk over a sub-strata of Lego.

While Polynesian navigators had to make do with charts made from sticks and string, knitting their way along, battling to turn the heel, we are equipped with the latest products of science which are designed to ensure that our destinations are always located on the fuzziest crease.

An old chart, with previous workings still unerased, is like a trip down memory lane, like the fond perusal of an old family photo album with dear old mum in her bumblebee bathing costume at Broadstairs.

In the days when we worked our tides it usually meant getting up at 4 am to chomp joylessly at a bacon butty in a silence broken only by the rasp of stubble. The chart would show ship's DR progressing in huge strides only to dissolve into a rook's nest of fixes and computations off the next headland. Studying the stained and cocoa-impregnated charts of previous years could teach one much. A passage which started with a fair stream and a gentle force 2–3 showed the navigator's art in its finest form. Working on a level chart table, untroubled by thoughts of his/her last meal, it showed meticulous workings, neat as a Victorian sampler blessing this happy house or the Lord's Prayer in cross-stitch.

As the weather deteriorated positions were recorded at longer intervals and finally not at all. The written log book followed a similar trend, recording the reefing of the mainsail, the rolling up of the jib and the starting of the plonker. 'Rffd mum stewed job eng on,' it read economically. On the chart all workings ceased upon sighting the first landfall. There followed another six hours of frantic banging around and peering through the binos before a final arrival and yet another cocoa ring.

Tidal considerations

Nowadays the powerful diesel auxiliaries of modern yachts combined with the 'waterproof integrity' of today's foul weather clothing means that the sailing family in their cockpit, zipped up, hooded and booted, are about as impregnable as a can of pilchards, and the yacht can be banged to windward in a permanent private Niagara. Foul tides can be ignored.

In the days of low hp petrol auxiliaries, when you had to clap your ear to the deck to tell whether they had stopped and which were as temperamental as operatic sopranos, all bust and bravura, you had to study your tides. Petrol auxiliaries dribbled highly explosive vapours into your bilges to produce gaff-rigged volcanoes, and a hot-line to heaven for those in a State of Grace – a dizzy descent for the rest. You had a straight choice of motoring while sniffing away like a bloodhound, or sailing and working tides.

Tidal currents run backwards and forwards, fast or slow and all are made plain in the Tidal Atlas, each page of which has a mass of tiny arrows going in all directions like wasps at a picnic. Navigators have a ritual called 'working out the tides'. 'One-hour-after-Dover, two-hours-after-Dover . . .' they intone, and so on until they are almost there when lady-wives hand them a mug of soup. Then they have to start again. They reach the same point. 'Bread?' say lady-wives.

Depth recording

Successful landfalls in the past depended upon log, lead and look-out – the latter being the cry of warning as the former was heaved and Percy stuck his great daft poll outboard to see what was going on. The heaving of the lead is now a forgotten art – save only for the scars remaining on the crosstrees, the busted glass in the forehatch and grandad's cauliflower ear.

The lead line was marked with the intention of generating utter confusion in the mind of the navigator. Bits of string, coloured rag and scraps of boot leather were stuck on at random intervals. If there wasn't a mark you called that bit a 'deep', an absurdity of some magnitude since you couldn't *measure* it. The leadsman/woman stood by the rail, coiling, hurling, cursing and coiling again and again, becoming soaked from the waist down.

Let us watch a typical man-and-wife team as they approach land in the fog. The MUG is on the helm, conning wife and ship. His eyes are narrowed in concentration, he's no mug, he's dry.

'You'd better tack NOW!' lady-wife growls, dripping. She takes a heave. 'Mark-a-quarter-less-five,' she hails correctly, 'Deep four . . . mark three . . . mark, don't-blame-me.' CRASH. They hit the beach as if heading an invasion.

The invention of the echo-sounder has altered all that. Humming away like a bee in a jam-jar, depth can be read at a glance. That is, provided the instrument is kept down below in a dark corner as if ripening green tomatoes. Up on deck in the sunlight, where it is really needed, you can't see pussy.

'Go down and see what the echo-sounder says,' father tells Percy. The lad sits with his great red ear clamped to it.

'What have you got?' demands father, eyeing the fast approaching river bank.

'Earache' grieves Percy as the ship lurches to a stop.

GPS navigation

GPS, or 'Great Purple Snakes' as this form of navigation is laughingly called, demands only the level of intelligence reached by chimps at a tea party. A small instrument privately consults satellites and then tells you where you are. It had better be right, mate, a GPS instrument with a flat battery is about as cheery as the rearlights of the last bus home on a wet Sunday night.

GPS navigation is based upon establishing WAY-POINTS along the intended route and then with jib rolled and main strapped in, motoring flat out from one to another. It is like a supermarket trolley-dash (all baked beans and no booze). It offers all the challenge of a join-the-dots competition. The rougher the going gets, the harder they bang along. The yacht vibrates like some obscure form of orthopaedic treatment.

'Stttttart Ppppppoint Abbbbbeam!' pronounces father with pride, dewlaps a'quiver and the peak of his cap visible only as a blur.

The passage plan

This is worked out in advance of going to sea and calls for a good deal of luck and the imagination of Mystic Meg.

The navigator has not the slightest idea what is going to be happening in Fairisle, Rockall, Bailey and SE Iceland or whether the kennels will be able to accommodate Bonzo. He/she works at home between the marmalade and the tomato sauce under the baleful eye of a spouse, who won't warn him a second time . . .

Passage plans will go down in history as some of the great works of fiction. Working with tidal atlases, pilot books and a crystal ball the size of the dome of St Paul's, the navigator plots a course around a line of waypoints like a game of rounders, with the object of reaching the lock gates just as they creak open.

Having lingered over breakfast for more toast and another cup of coffee, they blow the whole thing by starting two hours late.

Pilot books

The joint influences of shipping forecast and Admiralty Pilot Book combine to produce a sense of stark foreboding. Pilots written by and *for* yachtsmen are more soothing altogether and mention things like lovely views and tearooms, but your Admiralty Pilot aims to inspire respect and a sense of dread. If an anchorage happens to be even remotely attractive it gets the full treatment. It reads like a dirge:

'Ooooo!' it sorrows, 'Oooo there are dangerous overfalls in the approaches and Ooooo unchartered rocks in the entrance Oooooo!'

The yachtsman enters with beating heart. On no account, says the book, must Desperation Point be allowed to open up Sepulchre Bay. It is like entering a haunted house. Mother has only to bang a locker door shut and his little boots are treading thin air.

Some useful aids

Weather warnings

When seagulls swoop
You get covered in poop
When buttercups abound
You are hard aground

Storm warning

If your wife bangs pots and pans
Abandon any sailing plans.
Never mind the rising glass
If you're wise you'll cut the grass,
Mend the fence, unblock that drain
And soon you may make sail again.

When the wind is in the south you may live a life of slouth
When the wind is in the west put aside your flannel vest
When the wind is in the north, sell the boat and ★★★★ orf
When the wind is in the east, go consult your parish priest.

Wind and sea criteria based upon appetite afloat

Force 1–3   Cold chicken drumsticks and soggy lettuce. 'Oh yes please, make mine two and lots of that salad cream with the coloured bits in it that looks like Yuk!'

Force 3–4   'I'll have mine in the cockpit please, it's too nice to stay down below. Just the one drumstick. No salad cream.'

Force 4–5   Entire ship's company line the cockpit, each clutching a drumstick. They look like a team of hand-bell ringers. Crew take a keen interest in the navigation and religion, eg 'Ohhhhh, how long before we get there for God's sake?'

Force 5–6   Exhilarating. 'By Harry we'll remember this, eh! Just a Cream Cracker, Doris, no (gulp) butter and no (gulp) cheese.'

Force 6–7   'Nothing for me . . . hang on to Percy's belt . . . Awww!'

Force 7 plus '. . . and I hope you'll take the trouble to listen to the forecast next time, Norman. I told you, didn't I . . . DIDN'T I, Norman?'

Rules of the Road

The Traffic Separation System is closely similar to a motorway ashore and similar rules apply:
If you wish to stay in the motorway
The only way to survive
From the moment you enter
Stay bang in the centre
At a steady fifty-five.

Sailing Rules

Stay on port tack don't go about
Let him on starboard chicken out.
He's on the wind you're on the run
Standing on is much more fun.
Don't give way when overtaking
Let the other do the braking.
Under engine you've right of way
If on your port bow t'other lay
But if she's on your starboard bow
Then just ignore the silly cow.
When two lights you see ahead
One of green and one of red
And above two more, both white as well
Turn right around and go like hell.

Running aground

Running aground is inseparable from navigation. The following notes will be of particular interest to the Trouts.

There are several unmistakable indications when a boat runs aground. If she is towing a dinghy it hits her right up the stern as if scoring a penalty kick, at the moment of impact the entire crew bob a curtsey as if kissing the Bishop's ring and bend at the knees in an 'evening-all' gesture. The helmsman will go galloping forwards still clutching the tiller.

A typical case

It takes more than a black eye-patch and an inflatable parrot to make an old sea-dog – and even sea-dogs can run aground. It will not be father's fault but neither will mother tolerate the use of that word in front of the children.

When a yacht goes aground it is a case of bum-up-bows-down like some rural dowager being presented at court. The Boy up forward, looking for whimbrels, soars over the pulpit and Bosco down below, spouting tea, rockets forward into the loo. There is a crash of broken porcelain. Everybody calls out 'We're aground!' thus making it official.

'I see you've gone aground then,' notes a passing yachtsman intuitively. It is a kindly inquiry and made with smiling good humour. It is a pity that he happens to be riding a bike.

If it happens on the ebb the yacht settles rapidly in a series of lurches – like a village hall ballerina in a crepe paper tutu and baking foil wings doing her dying swan to rapturous applause and creaking floorboards.

Getting her off

Initial attempts made with engine screaming astern, the backing of jibs and poking with spinnaker poles may fail. If the yacht went on with the wind dead astern a heavy gybe-all-standing, which is known as 'trepanning', may do the trick with a bonus crop of bobble-caps thrown in.

In the old days of bogey stoves and bumkins a gaffer owner could dip his peak, ruck his throat, trice his tack and boot the cat. The modern yacht offers a different course of action. Here are some of the options:

All run forward
All run from side to side

All jump up and down

All pile into the dinghy to lighten-ship

The latter option is certain to prove effective and the yacht, with her engine still flat out astern, will last be seen ten miles off Clacton and going like the clappers while her crew are being rescued by grinning lifeboatmen.

You may think that a twin-keeler is the answer to the problem of grounding and that she'll be sitting up there like the Arc de Triomphe or a bandy-legged goalkeeper (take your pick), with her crew waiting in comfort for the returning tide. If you think that, then I'm Miss Muffet.

You are more likely to be stuck on a steep mud slope at a funny angle, all huddled down below on the up-hill side, while father with a teaspoon on a string as a plumb-bob mournfully aligns it with a crack in the loo door. The rain hammers on the deck. Daringly you pick up a Scrabble tile. 'DON'T MOVE!' he squeaks. Very nice that is. Oh very nice I'm sure.

If other methods fail you may try kedging. The kedge anchor on a long bit of rope must be rowed out by dinghy and 'laid' at maximum scope in the direction of deep water. What happens is this: father (whose name is Macnamara and the leader of this sorry band), who is the most technically advanced of the crew *and* has the certificate to prove it, gets into the dinghy and with paddles threshing struggles the boat about thirty or forty feet distant. By the time he has shipped his paddles, grasped the kedge, thrown it overboard and untangled the rope, he is back alongside again. Howling valuable instructions he tries again and again, finally settling for what he can get.

Now it is all hands together, lads, heave away handsomely. Let's have a shanty someone. The anchor ploughing smoothly through the mud comes home like a toy horse on a string, bringing with it a marine biologist's paradise of low life, weed, mud and reeking slime.

Once you are totally and irrevocably stuck, why then you must endeavour to salvage what you can of your dignity – a prospect about as effective as donning a hospital examination smock, slit up the back like a broad bean.

There will most likely be a procession of passing yachts whose crews will beam happily and tell you that 'you're on then', or in the case of fishermen with £££s in their eyes: 'Narsty ole spot you'm on there squire,' offering 'a pluck off afore it's too late, seein' as 'ow the moon's on the wane.'

Adopt a mien of faintly laconic amusement, give a languid wave. You often come here . . . Or you may resort to cunning and pretend that you are there for a scrub. You often sail two miles out of the estuary and stick her down in the middle of an acre of stinking, popping, hissing ooze. Whatever you do, though, *don't be tempted to walk ashore* for a bite to eat and to do a bit of shopping.

If you do this, why then you will blow it. You will leave your return until too late, which can be tragic, yes *tragic*, I tell you. The returning tide will come galloping in, gurgling and trickling over the mud with a scum of plastic beakers and defunct crabs. Your small band will break into a shambling trot.

They cannot beat it. Tidal experts rapping calculators can show that tidal height above the mud is exactly equal to height of welly when the wearer reaches a position 12 ft (3 m 657.6 mm) from the boat.

Miriam in her shorty boots and wearing jeans too tight to permit rolling (and she's damned if she's going to take them off) will have to be given a piggy-back, and there's a nice sight for you.

Let us end this small volume on a note of hope. As the day wanes and evening paints the sky in pastel hues, as the lonely heron rows his weary homeward way, our little band of friends plod seawards across the nacreous mud. They are led by Gerald who is cursing roundly in strangled tones, the arms of his fair jockey around his throat. Beneath his chin she is holding a bottle of milk and a sliced Hovis – toothsome fare to speed his flagging boot-steps. And so let us leave them, heading into the sunset at the end of a long and eventful day.

Who knows what further adventures lie in wait?